INSIDE THE US NAVY SEALs

Gary Stubblefield

with

Hans Halberstadt

This book is dedicated to my best friend and wife, Suzie

First published in 1995 by Motorbooks International Publishers & Wholesalers, 729 Prospect Avenue, PO Box 1, Osceola, WI 54020 USA

Library of Congress Cataloging-in-Publication Data
Stubblefield, Gary.
Inside the US Navy SEALs/Gary Stubblefield.
p. cm.
Includes index.
ISBN 0-7603-0178-6 (pbk.)
1. United States. Navy. SEALs. I. Title.
VG87.S76 1995
359.9--dc20 95-36496

On the front cover: A SEAL team member silently emerges from the ocean wearing a closed-circuit Draeger Mark V breathing apperatus. Toting his M-16, this SEAL is ready for a day at the beach. *Zone Five Photo*

On the back cover: The author, Commander Gary Stubblefield.

Printed and bound in the United States of America

Table of Contents

Acknowledgments

by Gary Stubblefield

Only a former career team guy could tell this story. But I am not a writer as so many of my associates can attest to. I could not have done it without the wide-ranging experiences and opportunity to work with all the professionals I knew throughout my career. More importantly, this book would not exist without the patience, guidance, and hard work provided by Hans Halberstadt. It simply is because of him that there are words on this paper. He helped sell the idea to Motorbooks International. He has made it readable, and if the reader finds it interesting, it is because of Hans. Many close associates and friends I worked with throughout my career provided me guidance and support during my active duty years, and they deserve recognition. While space does not permit my naming every one individually, I thank them all profusely.

RADM Ray Smith and RADM Tom Richards, along with three other officers, went through Basic Underwater Demolition/SEAL (BUD/S) Class 54 with me and each has achieved phenomenal success in their careers. The two admirals will guide the community into the year 2000 and beyond, and I thank them for their friendship and camaraderie throughout the years and pray they keep the community climbing that tough road full of never-ending obstacles. Wade Puckett and John Marsh taught me the ethics and importance of being a good operator during my first overseas tour to Vietnam. Wade's guidance probably kept me alive through many tough situations both in Vietnam and from his teachings in later years. Norm Carley became a close friend early in my career and while his style may differ from mine, we think pretty much the same. He is a proven commodity and remains a good friend and business partner. Steve

Grimes became one of the young SEALs I respected most in my BUD/S class and subsequent Vietnam and other area deployments. He has become like a brother over the past twenty-five years–and remains one tough customer even today. Gary Gallagher, my command master chief at SEAL Team Three, was my solid rock. He has always held that sixth sense of what to do both in combat and in administrative leadership roles. He continues to succeed in life after being a SEAL. Jim Gray has forgotten more about small combatant craft operations than I'll ever learn. He is a legend in the boat community and a Naval Reservist to boot. Jim Kauber, my command master chief in the Persian Gulf for part of my tour there has continued to work closely with me in commercial security issues since our respective retirements from the teams. He is a true professional and gentleman. Tom Coulter and I first met in Korea and kindled an everlasting friendship. He is now a successful businessman enjoying the fruits of years of hard labor. George Hudak, now a warrant officer, is one of the best instructors I ever encountered and continues to ready our new prospective SEALs going through BUD/S with his wisdom, experiences, and patience. CPO Dave Billings, who passed away with a heart attack a few years ago, left his mark on many of us for having been the most competent combat swimmer ever to cross our quarter-deck. His legend and teachings will live on forever in our community at the heart of our mission. And to Margrethe Fuller, the "real" SEAL Detailer at the Naval Military Personnel Command who was my assistant and continues to be a close friend that can share similar insights in the community. Many thanks are owed to Mark Monday who finally got me off the dime to begin writing. He co-authored my first book, Killing Zone. Of course, the patience to allow me to work 12hr days in my job and then spend another several hours working on this book is a hallmark of Suzie, my wife. She has been a saint throughout the effort.

Preface

The US Navy SEALs, along with the Army's "Green Berets" are a microscopic element of the armed forces of the United States. There are very few of them. They represent no more than small change in the big budget of the Department of Defense (DoD). In many respects, these two closely related congregations of warriors are an archaic, obsolete, hopelessly romantic relic of a time and tradition long gone. In an age of intercontinental missiles, remote control and long range weapons, of invisible fighters and Mach 3 fighters, who really needs these little bands of riflemen? We do, as it turns out.

The SEALs are a small, cloistered brotherhood aloof from the Navy, the DoD, and civilian society. Applicants are accepted only after a long and arduous trial by water torture; once admitted to this little brotherhood, baby SEALs take a vow of silence; few ever discuss what they do and how they do it. It is a fairly new community, less than thirty years old.

Naturally, and inevitably, the people and the exploits of such a community fascinate the larger, excluded society. Americans first started hearing about the SEALs during the 1960s when they were identified by the Buzz Sawyer comic strip; their combat exploits intrigued many of us. But unlike the much larger Army "Green Beret" community, with its similar mandate and mission, we didn't hear too much about the SEALs. The missions were too tough for reporters to cover, for one thing, and the nature of the missions plus the tradition of silence kept the media at a distance.

The result, predictably, was a romantic, theatrical legend that has little to do with the real world and the real people in the teams. A lot of our information about SEALs comes from works of complete fiction, like the movie "US Navy SEALs." The few people who've emerged from careers in this business have generally told exaggerated war stories. While these stories are sometimes true, they tend not to tell the whole story. Ask a former SEAL what he really did on the teams and he'll likely say, "I can tell ya–but then I gotta kill ya!"–embellished with a dramatic snicker and wink.

Gary Stubblefield is one of the first naval officers to make a cradle to grave career in the SEALs and Naval Special Warfare. He fought in Vietnam and commanded SEAL Team Three, Special Boat Squadron One, and Task Unit PACIFIC in the Persian Gulf. Unlike many officers who used time in the SEALs as a kind of career "ticket punch" qualification as a warrior to gain rank, Gary has dedicated his professional life to the teams and their missions.

He is unusual (if not unique) in that he's what people in special ops call an "operator;" that is a man who actually has heard the sound of guns fired in anger, somebody who goes on missions, takes the risks, and who has the experience of being way out on the very pointy end of the spear. You'd think such operators would be common in the senior ranks of the Naval Special Warfare community–but that's not the case any more; few of the current commanders or senior staff at Coronado, California, where Naval Special Warfare is based, have any direct experience with combat. And that's creating a problem.

Gary retired as a commander recently, but he's still part of the SEALs and Naval Special Warfare. And although he retired, he has never been *retiring*–he has opinions, ideas, moral commitments. His change of command/retirement speech was blunt, detailed, and politically incorrect. A senior chief who admires Gary greatly told me, gleefully, how Gary said some things that needed to be said, even if they hurt some feelings. Political correctness can be found just about anywhere, even in the US Navy SEALs. Gary, like other operators I know, doesn't swear much, doesn't exaggerate much, and doesn't beat around the bush on important issues. He upset his colleagues, even with his retirement speech. Maybe that's why he retired as a commander, rather than a captain.

Although retired from the active Navy, Gary is still intimately involved with SEAL operations and training. His company, a partnership employing other retired and reserve SEALs, develops training documents and procedures for use in Naval Special Warfare. He conducts studies of SEAL missions during operations in places like Grenada, Panama, the Persian Gulf, and elsewhere.

So here is the inside story of the US Navy SEALs, told by one of the first professional officers and operators to retire from a full career in the business of Naval Special Warfare.

–by Hans Halberstadt

I never dreamed about one day writing of my experiences as a Navy SEAL. In my years in the teams there were so many adverse experiences with the media types. Then after retiring in 1990, I began to see some of the books that were being written about our community and how so many of them failed to tell the story from what I consider to be a realistic perspective. Within some, I saw what could be termed sensationalism come into play–things that would tend to make the reader feel that we are a bunch of trigger happy, partying adventurists. My own perspective is that 98 percent of the SEALs are professionals; intelligent and responsible types who want to serve their nation in the way that best suits their personalities.

Then I encountered Hans Halberstadt. He had heard that I had done some consulting for Time-Life Books after retiring from the teams. He had plans to put together some unclassified informational readers about the SEALs and asked if I would be willing to assist. After getting to know him much better, I grew to not only like him personally, but more importantly, to trust and appreciate his ability to present as honest a portrayal as possible. Sometime during my helping him, we began to discuss the need for a book that told the SEALs' story from the inside out with an accurate perspective bringing out both the good points and those that are often not mentioned. He had the talent to write, and I had the experiences to write about. With a more than generous amount of time, he has over the past many months helped me to lay out a story that will not "tell all" or serve to be an expose; but rather to say what hasn't been said in other books; to let those readers interested in knowing what it is like from the inside to be a Navy SEAL.

I hope that my teammates will see and feel some of themselves in the writings of this story–and that they don't get too thin-skinned when I bring up some of my personal perceptions or observations of events or policies that were not carried out right or were not promulgated as I think they should have been. I also hope that in some areas, some of the lessons learned over my career might one day guide a planner or help one of my fellow SEALs out of a tight spot or prevent the loss of life. At the same time, I hope that those readers that are not familiar with the SEALs or those who might be interested in becoming a SEAL or supporting the SEALs in some manner, shape, or form will come away with a greater respect and understanding for what I believe are the best trained and most competent individuals in the US military today.

First, a brief run through my resume before introducing you to the wet and wonderful world of the SEALs.

I was commissioned in 1969 at the University of Idaho, and my first assignment as a new ensign was to Class 54 at what was then called UDTRA Underwater Demolition Training at Coronado. Among my officer classmates in 54 were Ray Smith and Tom Richards, both of whom have gone on to command Naval Special Warfare (NSW) forces as rear admirals in charge of NAVSPECWARCOM, the US Navy's Special Warfare Command. Class 54 was, in fact, studded with people who later went on to great accomplishments in NSW. The pre-training program began in June, and the class survivors graduated in January 1970.

I was assigned to SEAL Team One upon graduation. My first assignment there was to take thirty five enlisted guys, ranking E-5 and below, to the Army's jump school at Ft. Benning, Georgia. That was my first leadership role outside of training, and it was fun; they were good guys, and we had a good time–although it was *cold* there at Benning. Then it was back to SEAL Team One and a slot in *Kilo* Platoon commanded by LTJG John Marsh. Kilo was then preparing to go to Vietnam by pre-deployment training. The platoon was without a chief petty officer at the time but did have the services of an experienced leading petty officer, PO1 Wade Puckett. Wade was one of those legendary characters you hear about in the SEALs, a guy who'd been to Vietnam already seven times; this was to be his eighth and last tour there.

We deployed in June of 1970 and operated down in the southern part of Vietnam–more about that later.

I came back to take over as assistant diving officer and then relieve Michael Horst as an SDV (SEAL Delivery Vehicle, a kind of wet mini-submarine) platoon commander for SEAL Team One. I stayed with the team until 1972, then went to Korea as the UDT advisor to the Korean Navy. After that three-year tour I came back to take over as research and development, test and evaluation (RDT&E) officer for Special Warfare Group Two, where I stayed for two years and helped develop the Mk 15 Swimmer Life Support system and numerous combat swimmer weapons systems. Then it was off to become executive officer (XO) for SEAL Team Two–the last of the lieutenant-grade XOs for the SEAL teams, another topic for later discussion. Then it was on to Naval Postgraduate School, followed by a tour as the first NSW career placement officer and detailer.

Then it was off to a unique group called the Special Development Unit. I participated in that for three years–and I won't tell you the details of that later, but I will talk about some of the lessons learned there. Then it was off to take command of SEAL Team Three from 1986 to 1988. I went from there to take command of a SEAL task unit in the Persian Gulf during Operation Earnest Will in 1988. Then it was back to take over Special Boat Squadron One. Two months after completing my hitch as commander of Special Boat Squadron One I retired, in January of 1990. I started two companies to provide consulting services to NSW and other clients–both government and commercial–businesses I still operate today.

Now, that brief resume doesn't sound very dramatic but it is a typical tour for a professional Navy officer in today's SEALs. And since I was one of the very first officers to actually spend my whole career in the SEALs, I have some observations about this little community that come from a rather unusual perspective. That's partly because the profession of SEAL officer is a relatively young one (a little over twenty-five years); it is also because we are constrained, while still serving, from providing detailed information about what SEALs do and how they do it . . . constraints that largely disappear after retirement.

But if you think I am going to spin a bunch of wild, angry war stories about the SEALs you are wrong. As a professional naval officer, as a professional member of the tiny fraternity we call Naval Special Warfare, I feel a strong sense of loyalty to, and respect for, the people who served with me in the past, the people who serve now, and those men who will follow us later.

Loyalty makes two demands: one is to keep quiet, to keep secrets– especially the ones about highly classified information; but loyalty also demands that you speak up when something needs saying. As one of the first professional SEALs to retire after a full career in the new community, as somebody who's watched the Naval version of Special Warfare evolve over the decades, and as somebody with experience in a wide range of combat environments, I have some strong opinions about our legendary little community–where it has been, where it is going.

While most Americans have heard about the US Navy SEALs, not many people really know who we are, what we do, what we are good for, where we fail. Mostly that's our own fault. We've purposely kept the public at arm's length, partly for genuine security reasons, partly because it seems to somehow enhance the legend. And we are funny about our legend– we make a big deal about keeping a low profile, then walking around San Diego wearing ball caps and T-shirts emblazoned with *US Navy SEAL* on them or order personalized license plates for our cars that denote our units. That's an issue we need to discuss.

There have been other books written about our SEAL community but usually from the perspective of the outsider, or they've been fictional accounts that dramatize or even invent elements of the story. And my associate Dick Marcinko's best sellers are part of this process, too; all these books are accurate about certain small elements of what SEALs are and what SEALs do, without ever telling the whole story as it looks to people in the community. We do some things extremely well, some things we have done extremely badly. So here's a different kind of book about special warfare, US Navy-style, a look *inside the US Navy SEALs.*

–*by Gary Stubblefield*

CHAPTER 1

One Foot in the Water

We in the SEALs, Special Boat Squadrons, and the Naval Special Warfare community are the United States' *small unit maritime special operations force.* We don't generally and should not operate in units larger than sixteen men. We don't do multi-platoon operations–although we've been pressured to try, and we haven't been successful with the attempts. By keeping the units small we are able to avoid large force operations; we don't operate as companies, multiple platoons, and certainly not as a whole team. Our niche, our mandate, is to be extremely good at very small unit operations. In fact, our best ops are conducted with a squad of only eight men–or fewer! A tiny unit like that is hard to detect, easy to command and control, and perfectly suited to many kinds of critical combat operations.

We like to say that we try to always keep one foot in the water. While you may sometimes see Green Berets doing operations in the water and even being launched and recovered from submarines, their missions are typically inland. Ours, on the other hand, are–or should be–in, through, or adjacent to the water. We plant explosives on targets from under water; we recon harbors, beaches, and target vessels; we emplace mines underwater using our own little submarine, the SDV (SEAL Delivery Vehicle); we use the water as an insertion medium to reach assigned land targets. These are all missions for which we are uniquely trained, tasked, and equipped.

We are part of a larger community of warriors, the Special Operations Command (SOC). Our brothers in arms are the Army's Special Forces (a.k.a. the Green Berets), the Rangers, the Nightstalkers special aviation unit, and the Air Force's Special Operations Wing (SOW). Each organization has its own bag of tricks and special talents, a lot of which overlap. We train to do recon and deep strike missions, for example, that are properly the primary job of Rangers or Green Berets–but also jobs we may find tasked to us because the target is close to the water, for example, and we are better able to execute the insertion or infiltration part of the mission than the other units.

SEALs and NSW have two major assignments: we perform missions to support special operations, where we work for a joint commander in a SOC theater, and we work for the Navy's conventional amphibious task force commander–a conventional operation using special ops units, equipment, and techniques.

That's the overview. But what are we really good at?

Direct Action and Strike Missions

We are generally quite good at maritime "direct action" missions, the operations where we go out as a little unit and blow up a ship, take down a target, capture a prisoner or conduct reconnaissance. We did this a lot in Vietnam and in the Persian Gulf; it takes real-world practice and experience, and when we get that experience, we are very good at this mission.

Foreign Internal Defense (FID) Missions

We are extremely good, though seldom used, for the kind of foreign internal defense mission–training members of foreign armed or paramilitary forces–traditionally performed by the Army's Green Berets. When we get a chance to teach our skills to sailors in other navies or maritime paramilitary forces, we "force-multiply," and we achieve extremely good results from it! While not all of us are good at living in other cultures, eating foreign food, and speaking a foreign language, we have done it in Vietnam, Korea, Kuwait and the Gulf, and Central America, and we are beginning to do it in the old Soviet Union.

Long Term Ops

We are capable of doing long range, long term combat operations, but we are typically not very good at them. That's because on such operations we tend to lose the ability to be fast, light, and mobile...we often then require external support forces. As soon as we, or anybody else, starts humping 100lb rucksacks, the ability to do what SEALs have traditionally done best–very fast, very light, mobile operations disappears. One of the exceptions was during Vietnam when we worked with the Australian Special Air Service (SAS) on occasion for week-long long range patrols.

That's what we learned to do in Vietnam, and I was part of that early learning curve. It was a different mission than the Navy's UDT "frogmen" had been doing, but we worked out a niche for ourselves that made a lot of sense then, and a lot of sense today. Let me tell you about what it looked like to a young SEAL officer at the beginning of the modern SEAL era.

Gary Stubblefield's One Foot in the Mud

Kilo Platoon of SEAL Team One, with John Marsh in command, went over to Vietnam in the summer of 1970. SEALs were then tasked with an interesting role, very different from the role they are tasked with today. We conducted direct action missions–ambushes of small units of Viet Cong (VC) soldiers, tax collectors, and enemy logistics support infrastructure. Until the SEALs came along down in the Mekong Delta, these enemy units could do pretty much what they wanted, particularly at night. Nobody had the training, aptitude, equipment, motivation, or mission to take them on, so they were ignored, and they had, as a result, beaten our side in the opening battle of the campaign to win the delta.

We went to work and, believe me, we really kept one flipper in the water all the time. Many of the platoons from SEAL Teams One and Two performed as many as 100 or more 'wet' operations in a six month period. Out of my own roughly fifty five personal ops over there, only three didn't involve getting wet. We got wet getting off the boat, we got wet sitting in rice paddies, we got wet wading through the canals.

We went after the VC mostly, with occasional missions against, or encountering, North Vietnamese Army (NVA) units or their support units. Our platoon's base was a subtenant aboard a Vietnamese and US Riverine compound and that was handy because the riverine units sometimes provided support. And we had our own indigenous Kit Carson scouts (enemy soldiers who'd changed sides or Cambodians that came down as sort of mercenaries) and LDNN (the *Lin Dai Nui Nai*, a Vietnamese SEAL-type unit) people attached directly to our platoon.

There wasn't anything fancy about the ops; if we heard that a VC unit or a tax collector would move along a certain route on a specific night, we'd go out and attempt to set a trap for them. If we knew a VC leader was in a particular hooch, we'd go try to grab him. We didn't score all the time, but we made a few points, and this had also a psychological impact on the VC.

We did best, I think when we captured one of their guys, got information from him, then went back into their areas and captured their weapons and supplies. We had a lot of success with that.

The rules changed almost daily. In fact, just before I left we were ordered to not fire unless fired upon–a great way to be killed first! The stupidity of this kind of rule became one of the lessons learned during the war, applied to our modern operations.

The KISS Principle

But one basic rule of our own was to "keep it simple stupid." When we went out on an op we took a basic load of ammunition, a lot of water, and normally little or no food. We planned to stay no more than 24-48hr. We carried almost the same weapon we carry today, the M16 or AR15, with the then-new thirty-round magazine. Most of the rifles on the squad had a 40mm grenade launcher attached. The M60 machine-gun, in a cut-down version similar to the light version of today, and the 5.56mm Stoner provided high volumes of fire. We usually carried pistols, too, but only for prisoner control and last-ditch survival. We went over with just a couple of seabags worth of gear a piece and stayed for six months. Today a similar deployment will take over forty times that volume of gear on a man-for-man basis.

Launching the Mission

Patrol Ops Objectives, Plans

Our first objective was to go out and collect information about the enemy–"intelligence," we call it in the military. Second, we went out to try to stop what they were doing, sometimes by 'interdicting' them. Third, we went hunting for enemy soldiers to be captured alive and who could provide information for us. Even when we captured enemy who didn't talk, there was an element of doubt planted in the minds of his buddies in the VC–they couldn't know for sure if he was talking or not, and that doubt slowed their operations. Despite the popular impression of what we do, SEALs avoid blowing away every enemy they encounter–it's not good business. Here's a typical interdiction/ambush mission, the kind we did then and the kind we still do today.

When we got information that the VC were operating in a specific area we'd plan an op against them. There were usually a lot of choices because in our area there just wasn't anybody else stopping them. We began by collecting all the information we could on the general mission op area–where people moved, when they were active–typically at night, but sometimes at certain hours like midnight or just before dawn. If we came up with at least two confirming reports on an enemy unit's routine and activities, we would normally mount an op against it.

Once we had an idea of where we wanted to go, and when, we needed a closer look. On occasion that would come from US Air Force (USAF) photo-recon aircraft with their high resolution cameras, or we might just fly out in a Navy Seawolf helicopter gunship and take a look from the air for ourselves. This kind of deliberate planning lasted one or two weeks and was mixed in with all the other activity of the teams and the intel shop, part of a continuous process of planning, executing, and recovering from missions.

The mission cycle began about a day before departure. For starters, none of us went to the bar or had anything to drink. Not only did we need clear heads, we were just too darn busy. After evaluating the target I'd decide how many men to take, normally no more than six. We studied the maps, photographs, the intel reports; we prepared all our weapons and web gear; we checked for availability with the helicopter pilots; we coordinated with the boat crews who would deliver and extract us. The helicopters were scheduled, normally to provide gunship fire support and as an alternative extraction option if Plan A fell apart.

The boats were scheduled at the same time, the specific kind of craft dependent on the nature of the mission–and what was available at the time. Then the helicopter pilots, the boat crews, and the Vietnamese and US artillery were all briefed. The Army of the Republic of Vietnam (ARVN) artillery unit would be alerted, at the last minute, that we were going out and would operate in one of five or six grid squares; we wanted them to avoid shelling us by accident, to be ready to support us if we called, and to especially not tell their pals in the VC where we were going to be. And since we were going to be awake and busy for a solid 24hr during the op, we needed to get some sleep before the launch.

Once all the ducks were in a row I briefed my team. These briefings lasted an hour or hour and a half, max, a far shorter time than is normal today. That's because we all were already familiar with all the standard operating procedures (SOPs) and we already knew the area, all we needed to cover was the specific information pertinent to this particular operation. We had all worked together for a long time, before the deployment and since, and we knew the basic drill. Even so, I might remind the men to do things as subtle as filling their canteens with water or not using soaps with a noticeable odor or anything that might give us away by smell; we needed to go out ready to blend into the woodwork. The critical part, the area we concentrated on, was the component of the briefing format called *Actions at the Objective.*

Typically, we'd leave after dark and insert sometime around midnight. There were lots of ways for us to get into our area of operations (AO); we could drive to some, but didn't; we could go in on Medium SEAL Support Crafts (MSSC), which wasn't very sneaky; helicopters could drop us off, but that's not subtle either; or we could use the same little boats the locals used–the best way. With the Medium SEAL Support Craft (MSSC) or the helicopter, everybody for miles says, "Hey, here come the SEALs!" But when you come chugging up the canal in the same little sampan everybody's accustomed to, with Vietnamese at the helm, you tend to blend into the traffic and disappear.

SEAL ops invariably require boats for support. Back then we used the aforementioned MSSC and the Light SEAL Support Craft (LSSC). The MSSC was a good boat; the LSSC wasn't. It had a water-jet "Jacuzzi" drive that frequently clogged. Finally, we took the little Boston Whalers–good, reliable craft. But perhaps the best boat available was the one the Vietnamese already used, the sampan.

The US Navy doesn't commission sampans, you have to go get your own. My platoon leader, John Marsh, got ours on an op in a river near the U Minh forest. John found a boat moving along the river, loaded down with a VC taxman and money. "We'll take that, thanks," said John. Even with the bullet holes and stains, it was a good, serviceable boat with a reliable engine and room for a squad of SEALs. That was my first lesson in the idea that if you look like the locals, act like the locals, and think like the locals you can have a much greater level of safety and freedom in a dangerous place. You get away with a lot more if you look like a local and not a Mk 1, Mod 0 US Navy SEAL.

Insertion

It didn't take very long, or very many gun fights with the VC to figure out how to get SEALs in and out of the objective area more or less intact and unseen. At first, SEALs essentially barged up the rivers and canals during daylight. That didn't work too well. We learned to work at night, first with the standard Navy-issue boats and later with the indigenous water craft. We learned to insert in invisible places and unpredictable ways. We learned to move silently, set up an ambush, and wait for prey. Here's what we learned:

Darkness and rain are your friends and allies when they blind your enemies. We traveled at night, guided mostly by radar and experience, up the rivers and canals. We learned to throttle the engines back and to sneak, invisible and inaudible, into the enemy's back yard.

To further confuse anybody who might see us, the boat normally made numerous false insertions before and after the actual insertion, nosing the bow in to shore for a few seconds. To any VC watching it looked like we were coming ashore; I always hoped lots of VC squads lost plenty of sleep looking for us SEALs at those false insertions sites.

When we finally we got to the real insertion point, the MSSC or Patrol Boat Riverine (PBR) or whatever boat we were in would be eased into the shore, all weapons with chambered rounds and with the "pucker factor" right up around 100 percent. The boat crew manned all the weapons stations and everybody was primed to get hit at this extremely vulnerable moment. We clambered off the boat, invariably into the water or the mud. Of all my insertions, only three let me stay dry. Then we staggered ashore as silently as possible, loaded down with our gear–plus a few pounds of mud, water, and leeches, and on one occasion a snake wrapped around the rear security's leg.

Movement to the Objective

Now we formed up into patrol order, with the point man leading, followed by me and the rest of the group, with the rear security man (usually called the "tail-gunner") bringing up the rear. Unlike in the movies and in today's training, movement to the ambush site was often extremely slow. You sometimes moved only 100 meters in an hour; that's not very exciting in a movie, but it is quite exciting enough for me when it is enemy country and when there is a choice between killing someone or being killed yourself.

Out on Patrol

SEALs became, toward the end, an organization that developed the ambush to an art form. In fact, it was the focus of our operations. It isn't a glamorous or heroic kind of op, and some people found the idea distasteful; we were (and still are) supposed to call this mission "interdiction," an early example of emergence into political correctness, US Navy-style. Regardless of what you call it, here's how it works:

We'd get a mission to go out to a specific spot where something was known to be happening with an assignment to collect information, kill, or capture enemy soldiers. A routine mission like that is a job for a squad of SEALs–seven men at that time, one officer and six enlisted. But the full squad was seldom available; somebody was on leave, at the hospital, or malingering, so more often you'd go out with just five people. That was okay, though, because our preference was to operate with as few people as possible; that minimizes noise and makes command and control easier and more effective. Since command and control was better, the squad's firepower was just about as effective; the volume might not be as large, but it was easier to put on target.

And we liked a lot of firepower! Among this little troop was one M60 machine-gun with its heavy bullet and good penetration, a Stoner machine-gun with its high rate of fire against groups of enemy, with the remainder of the squad carrying CAR-15 carbines. But only one of the men would carry just the rifle–the man on the point. The others carried CAR-15s with XM148 or XM203 40mm grenade launchers attached. (The contest between the two experimental 40mm grenade launchers was won by the M203, used by the teams and other units today.)

Fire Support

We had three kinds of fire support available. First and foremost was from the boats that provided our direct support, the special boat units dedicated to riverine ops and SEAL missions. These MSSCs, LSSCs, and Boston Whalers all had a mix of machine guns, an 80mm mortar modified to provide direct fire, an early version of the Mk 19 grenade launcher, and sometimes a rotary mini-gun with a very high rate of fire. There were LAAWs–light anti-armor weapons–that were seldom fired; during more recent operations, these LAAWs were found to have become defective in accuracy. Those guys and those guns provided our first line of defensive firepower.

Second, we had our own US Navy helicopter gunships

overhead–light attack *Seawolf* versions of the UH-1H Huey with guns and rockets. These gunships were very good, were flown by highly dedicated crews, and would "scramble" in a heartbeat and come in through almost any kind of ground fire to help us. Every time we went out on an operation we made sure they were either overhead or knew where we'd be–and knew what our call-signs were, and what frequencies we'd be using.

Third, there were the conventional tube artillery fire bases within range of our area of operations (AO). We sometimes advised these units of our operations and asked to be worked into their fire support plans. But you had to be careful with them because the Vietnamese artillery units were badly infiltrated with VC and, without special precautions, this kind of coordination could be advertising your intentions to the opposing side. Part of our learning curve on this happened early during our tour; on our first two full up operations we were ambushed both times, and prior coordination or information leaks within the local Vietnamese units seemed to be the weak, dangerous link. We fixed that by either not telling them where we were going at all, or only telling them just at the last moment, as we were going out the door, so the VC didn't have time to set up on us. And that fixed the problem.

Finally, we could call on off-shore gunfire support from ships in range or from the riverine patrol forces or air cavalry units such as the Black Pony (which flew OV-10s) outside our organization. Either could provide fire support, but both could kill friendly forces accidentally, as happened from time to time.

The Kill Zone

Everybody's heard the expression, *some days you get the bear; some days the bear gets you;* well, plenty of SEALs have had the unhappy experience of being had by the bear and it is something we avoid by being as stealthy as possible. Once we ooze up to our ambush site, we insinuate ourselves into the woodwork. There are lots of ways to set up an ambush but the classic is the "L" shape, with the long part parallel to the trail or road and the short section at right angles, forming an interlocking field of fire. My position was normally in the center, and it was my role to trigger the ambush by firing at a crucial moment.

But an ambush is a lot like hunting–it IS hunting. You don't get to shoot until something comes by, and you have to make sure that you aren't shooting something "out of season." So we sit there, in our little hiding place, from about midnight until first light. This can be stunningly boring, uncomfortable work. We sit there, soaking wet, cold, in the gloom, waiting for a few trophy bad guys to amble down the trail. Instead, there might be honest fishermen heading off to a day working the nets, or a farmer headed to his fields. The latter we have to identify in the dark and refrain from shooting them, without revealing ourselves.

It can sometimes, be virtually impossible for everybody to stay wide awake and alert under these circumstances once the adrenal rush of the insertion and infiltration wears off. So we tie everybody together with a "tug line" that allows communication without noise. We can even let part of the team close their eyes for a few minutes at a time while a couple of men stay alert. If something comes hopping down the bunny trail, a tug on the line will bring everybody awake in a hurry.

So there is a lot more to an ambush than finding a comfortable spot along a river and waiting for somebody to come by. You need to find a suitable spot where you can hide five or six guys, then take on what can be a pretty sizable force of enemy. The best place for an ambush is generally a spot along a canal where there is a curve or a bend, an intersection of two canals, or where a trail meets the water. It is places like these where you can maximize your firepower, where you can have good cover and concealment, and where traffic volume suggests a good possibility of finding the enemy.

The ambush site needs to be suitable for insertion. You can't, for example, walk up a muddy or dusty trail in daylight because your footprints will give you away immediately. We try to come in to the site from the rear of the position, then position each man carefully for maximum potential. The machine-gunners need to cover the whole "kill zone" effectively. The riflemen need to be in position to engage point targets.

Spacing between men varies, normally based on terrain. In an open area we spread out a bit more for a bigger kill zone and to make us each harder targets; if the enemy counterattacks and you are all bunched together you become a lot easier to destroy. Along a sharp bend in a trail in the jungle, though, we are close together for concentrated firepower and better command and control. It all depends on terrain.

Two common things may trigger an ambush prematurely, sound and smell. The AK47 used by the VC and NVA was and is a terrific weapon, but the big safety on the rifle makes a very audible "klatch" as it is disengaged. If you are tippytoeing through the woods and suddenly hear a chorus of metallic clicks coming from the underbrush ahead, you are well advised to hit the dirt and fire toward the sound. This happened to a LOT of patrols in Vietnam. And the M16's safety makes its own distinctive, though quieter, warning click too.

Odor likewise provides ample warning to an alert enemy point man. Imagine a VC unit moving along a road where they know SEALs might operate; the distinctive smell of aftershave, for example, or a deodorant soap, or insect repellent, or a cigarette, could all provide a kind of warning of something that didn't fit into the normal routine. While no SEAL is dumb enough (with a few exceptions) to put smelly stuff on before an op, a lot of guys use the stuff as a skin conditioner; if you don't get it all off in the shower the smell can remain the next day.

There are lots of things like that which need to be considered. But as long as you're properly camouflaged, particularly at night, you can escape detection if you don't make noise and you smell just like the normal environment.

Being seen by the enemy wasn't such a problem at night over there with the plant life such as it was. But nowadays, I see many of the new operators wearing their linked ammo around their bodies. Guess they haven't realized yet that its like wearing dozens of little brass mirrors that even at night might give away the patrol, not to mention that the mud and foliage can more easily get onto them and create malfunctions.

Actually, there is one enemy that can probably find you no matter what: mosquitoes! They were so bad where we operated that they actually degraded our ops. We wore mosquito head nets to keep the clouds of them out of our eyes and noses, but if you are sitting still in the weeds, they orbit your position by the thousands with occasional kamikaze attacks by the most valiant of the bugs. The noise of these insects flying around your head, waiting their turn for breakfast, actually made it hard to hear a VC patrol walking up the trail in front of you. The mosquitoes were maddening!

Initiating An Ambush

Except in a dire emergency, the team waits for the signal to initiate the ambush. Typically, that is done by the patrol leader who waits until the enemy force is inside the kill zone. It is a job that takes some nerve and judgment, and if you make a mistake it can cost you all your lives. The way it usually works is that the patrol leader fires into the center of the enemy unit at a key target, or detonates the Claymore mine. When that happens everybody cuts loose. You need to be able to take the whole enemy force out entirely, quickly–or not take it on at all.

With just six men a SEAL ambush has somewhat limited

firepower and can't take on everything hiking down the trail. But we use demolitions and explosives in ambushes to enhance our firepower and to magnify the shock effect of the ambush when it is triggered. That's done with the M18 "Claymore" mine, an anti-personnel weapon that is "command-detonated" or fired with a hand-held electrical device. When the Claymore goes off several hundred steel ball bearings spray the kill zone like a dozen shotguns firing at the same time. It is devastating. Unless it is fired too early or late, or is pointed in the wrong direction (both a lot more common than you might think) a large number of enemy troops will be shredded by this excellent weapon. And any who are missed will be disoriented for at least a few seconds by the tremendous, unexpected noise of the blast.

That shock gives the six or so SEALs conducting the ambush a few precious seconds to finish off any survivors. The machine-gunner sprays down anybody standing and the whole area where the enemy unit is known to be. The riflemen take out individual targets–enemy soldiers they can see, either in the dim moon or starlight or by the enemy soldiers' muzzle flashes if they shoot back.

One really wonderful, sneaky thing SEALs learned to do in ambushes is to run a length of "det cord" (a form of high explosive that comes in rolls of 1/4in rope-like form) along ditches and other places where an ambushed enemy is likely to seek shelter from our firestorm. Seconds after the ambush is tripped, once the survivors have recovered and made a dive for the ditch with an intention of returning your fire, you pop the det cord. That pretty well demoralizes up the opposing team.

And it is real important to clean them all up. Unless you need a prisoner to take back for a visit with the guys in the Intel Shop, you have to ensure all the enemy are incapacitated. Just one can completely ruin your whole morning if he knows his business, recovers from the shock of the first contact, and elects to fight back. About the time you and the team stand up to congratulate yourselves he is likely to empty an AK magazine into your expedition, or maybe he'll toss a grenade into your little hiding place, now that he knows where it is. Not everybody turns and runs. There's usually one guy that gets mad and wants to get even. I recommend that nobody gives him the opportunity.

After initiating an ambush, we wait a few seconds, evaluate the results, then act accordingly. We will first set up a couple of guys for security, then send in a couple of other guys to police up the weapons and documents of the enemy force; they go back to the Intel shop for evaluation and to relate our account of the action. The ambushee's identity cards will reveal whether we actually got the VC leader we were after or if we merely took out a routine patrol of private soldiers. If we went after a target we want to know if we actually hit it.

Normally we will pull out of the ambush site after an engagement–but not necessarily. Sound doesn't travel far when you're in among the canals and the trees are thick. The sound of the ambush might not be audible for more than a few hundred meters. Maybe, if you're feeling lucky, you will elect to stick around. Maybe some more bad guys will dash up to see what the fuss is about; perhaps you can bushwhack them, too. This is called a "stay-behind."

Now, there are plenty of times when you won't fire a shot. Maybe the enemy doesn't cooperate by coming by. Maybe your radio quits working and you elect to not risk a fight with an enemy patrol-sized force because you can't call for the help that would otherwise be on call if you needed it. Or a whole platoon of NVA parade past; you could get a few but you wouldn't live to tell about the engagement. While the actual ambushes, when they happen, are incredibly exciting for everybody on both sides (although for different reasons), it is extremely common to sit out in the weeds all night and not fire a shot. Sometimes you'd see nobody at all. About the only things you can say about all the ambushes we did in the Mekong Delta that was really predictable were that you'd get wet, you'd be scared, you would also be extremely bored, and that the mosquitoes would eat you alive.

The ambush doesn't sound gallant, and it isn't. But it is the only way to take the fight to some kinds of enemy insurgent units in some kinds of places. It isn't for every kind of unit or every kind of man. It is, though, something at which the US Navy SEALs excel.

Extraction

So the sun could come up on six soggy, cold, leech-infested SEALs ready to go home. We would pick up the Claymore and the det cord, look around to make sure nobody was watching, then carefully move off to a new spot alongside the bank where–we sincerely hoped–the boat would come back to pick us up and get us back to the ranch. And that pickup spot would almost always be a different place than we used to get in since we or the boat might have been seen and somebody might have an ambush set up to ambush the ambushers!

Sooner or later the boat would materialize, nose into the bank, and we'd get wet and muddy again coming back aboard. The pucker factor for all hands would again be up over the red line while we were most vulnerable, but with the last guy aboard the coxswain reverses the boat back into midstream, then advances the throttles and gets us all out of Dodge. Although we could still get hit on the way back, and on occasion were, the danger and the pucker factor diminished quickly as we headed back to base.

E&E Plans - There if You Need Them

Escape and Evasion (E&E) plans are one of those things

that we usually pay scant attention to in our mission planning because, like wearing seat belts, we think we'll never need them. But we stick them in anyway since the standard five paragraph patrol leader's order calls for them. And we have heard the stories of when some distant SEAL in the past might have needed one. Basically these are merely a last ditch plan that makes sure each patrol member knows how to get home in the event everything is going down the tubes and the original plan isn't working. For example, we get shot off the beach and the boats can't come in to pick us up; we might decide to swim to sea four miles and meet a submarine at midnight.

During one situation where I had been training indigenous to perform a special over-the-beach operation, I became particularly close to some of them. In fact one of them took to me rather strongly–to the point that he even decided to get a haircut the same as mine. Well, being follically challenged, I sport no hair at all. This young man shaved his head just prior to his squad going out on a tough real-world mission.

They launched on their mission late at night and went up on the beach. Once ashore the patrol leader got scared and things started to fall apart. Somehow he made the determination to pull out and leave some of the operational gear. He and all but my buddy with the shaved head made it back to the beach and called in the boat for extraction and returned to the launchbase. Of course, we were not pleased with the Patrol Leader for leaving one of his men on the beach. During the mission planning I had insisted on an E&E plan that was simple. Merely move to a long stretch of beach north of the operational area and at midnight each night, come out to the water's edge and signal skyward and seaward with a red lens flashlight a series of Sierra's (dot-dot-dot) for about 10 minutes. We, in turn, had a small helicopter that could fly at night and would look for the signal. Of course its more complicated than that. For example, if the enemy had captured the party and then extracted information as to the signal, they could deceive the rescue party into coming in for a pickup and get ambushed themselves.

My little friend kept his head and did what the plan called for. At midnight the next night, our helo was flying low down the coast line. They saw the red lens light and were hesitant to come in for the pickup until they watched the evadee take off his hat, and they recognized the bald head. That was bonafides enough to come down and pick him up. The lesson learned here is not necessarily to shave your head but to have a workable E&E plan and to have some sort of recognition signal for the rescuers to know its legitimate.

Back at the Ranch

No matter how stressful the op might have been, the first thing done on return is a debriefing session with the intel specialists. Then the weapons and other personal equipment are cleaned and made ready for the next op–or the next emergency, which could materialize at any moment. Finally, it is off to the club–no matter how humble, there's always a club–for a drink, some chow, and some sleep.

The legend of the SEALs seems to emphasize a lot of drinking, and, for some people at some times, this was true. But few SEALs got involved in the drug culture that seemed to infect some parts of the "brown water" Navy during the later years of the war while I was in Vietnam. It was quite common for many sailors to drink heavily and use marijuana and harder drugs, too. Our people were more disciplined than that. I know some of our guys got into that, too, but, when discovered, they were quickly bounced from their units; there was no room for that kind of thing. Even today, it is automatic removal of the designator at a minimum if there is even minor evidence that one is involved in any drugs.

CHAPTER 2

SEAL Operations–the Good, the Bad, and the Ugly

Vietnam was such a large, dramatic, pivotal part of the history of US Naval Special Warfare, the US Navy SEALs and me, too, that it deserves more attention. The experience shaped, tempered, and improved us all.

SEAL missions became a lot more diverse than even President Kennedy would have imagined. We were always a tiny contingent in the grand scheme of battle but with an influence greater than that of most division-sized conventional units. We ran the coastal interdiction missions, with and without the Vietnamese. We learned to ferret out the enemy infrastructure, their tax collectors, their guerrilla commanders, their logistics support people, and their facilities. We found ways to cut their lines of communication, particularly in the network of rivers and canals of the delta. Their safe houses weren't safe from us, and they knew it. We could hurt them without firing a shot, but we did a lot of shooting too.

Ambush Lessons Learned

SEALs still train for those same ambushes today but since so few people in the teams have ever been in combat some of today's procedures are unrealistic. For one thing, you just don't go very far or very fast. You hear briefings today where a patrol will plan to go 12km to their objective; that's silly. You might do it in training, but you don't move 5mi through enemy territory, particularly a maritime territory, with possible booby traps or indigenous presence, to set up an ambush.

We learned that you could expect to move only 100 meters

in an hour sometimes. You've got to keep noise under control. You have to be alert to the noises around you; be prepared to locate booby traps before they located you. The mud will slow you down; sometimes you'd be in water up to your chest. In fact, moving 100 meters in an hour might be pretty fast. If we had to go back to the same kind of place and do the same kind of mission, I think we'd do it just about the same way–the boats would be better, we'd wear lightweight-effective body armor; and our radios would be more compact, reliable, and more powerful, but everything else would be pretty much the same.

One of the differences people would want to try would be the "whiz-bang" high tech things. We had huge, heavy starlight scopes then; now we have light and compact little night vision goggles (NVG) today. Back then we wouldn't usually bother with the scopes, but today we might rely on them more. We have global positioning system (GPS) navigation systems today versus the compass and pace line then. Everything is smaller, faster, lighter today.

There would be differences in the way we operate but not necessarily improvements. For example, we seldom get to live in an area for a long period today while preparing to conduct operations. The Persian Gulf is an exception, but otherwise we don't get to understand the mission area with the same depth of familiarity and knowledge. We were in the Persian Gulf long enough to get real familiar with the people, the terrain, the culture, and the weather. That made for good operations.

Another difference today is "briefing overkill." I go to briefings that last 5-6hr! That's silly–the average Navy SEAL's brain can't absorb all that data. And that's for an operation scheduled for only a day or two. If you ask why they feel the need for such elaborate detail, the typical excuse is that all contingencies and details need to be covered. The real reason, I think, is that the briefer wants to make a good impression on the senior officer present . . . instead of the people who are going off on the mission. I'll bet that if you left the senior officers out of the audience, the briefings would soon shrink to an hour or so.

Train the Way You Fight

I will mention some odd developments in NSW today, as we go along–and these criticisms aren't meant to indicate that we're not good at our business; we're the best at what we do. But nobody goes through a career in a profession where life and death are the bottom line without having some strong ideas about how things ought to be. My perspective is based on my experience; somebody with different experience will see these things a different way.

Here's an example: while we like to say we keep one foot in the water, as a matter of policy, we don't always do that, and we sure don't train to do that. We talk about going deep and staying dry on some major kinds of ops–and, oddly, we spend a great deal of our training time ashore, working on dry land, staying warm and dry. Now, since we're the arm of SOC that gets in the water, don't you think we should put most of our efforts into being good in the water? I do. We aren't as good at those skills as I would like to see us.

Basic Load

If today's SEAL teams were actually planning and conducting real-world combat operations every day, I think you'd quickly see a lot of the "high-speed" gear get left back in the lockers. When you conduct frequent ops in the same general combat region you learn to simplify and lighten up. Our riflemen go out with 200 rounds in their load bearing gear quite often today; 140 rounds were plenty back in the days when SEALs actually got into prolonged fire fights. All those rounds slowly wear you down, they make you sink a little deeper into the mud, make you just a little more tired–a little slower to react when you make contact with the enemy.

We have vastly better gear today than ever before. The radios, weapons, clothing, web gear, boots, and all the other items of personal equipment are better than ever. They are so good, and so light, that we tend to try to take it all along with us instead of keeping things simple. I have stopped a SEAL going out on an op and put his rucksack on a scale–it weighed 110lb! For a three day operation! What's wrong with this picture? All you really need for a three day op is a couple of Meals, Ready to Eat (MRE), a reasonable amount of water, your weapon and ammunition–and that's it, let's go. Some extra batteries, a spare radio somewhere in the team, no more.

Who Needs the Navy SEALs?

Now, if you know much about special operations or about the Army's Special Forces, you might think we're just like the Green Berets. After all, we wear pretty much the same uniforms, carry the same weapons and equipment, and train to execute many of the same kinds of basic recon, strike, and interdiction missions. You see them doing swim ops and even locking in and out of submarines; you see us patrolling deep inland. What's the difference–and if there isn't any, what do we need SEALs for, anyway?

The Army's Green Berets are far more numerous, in part because their "tooth to tail" ratio of support personnel-to-operator is vastly more expansive than ours. Their units are bigger, their real-world missions much different, and their talents and traditions much more oriented to the "unconventional warfare" and FID mission than we are. They tend to be specialists; we tend to be generalists. Their real turf is inland, often working with large groups of indigenous personnel. Our turf is in the surf–and we tend more often to kill indigenous personnel when we encounter them on a mission. Green Berets learn the language and culture of other nations; we learn to say "stop" and "drop that weapon!" Green Berets are superb team leaders, or medics, or weapons specialists, or communications experts; we are *each* pretty good medics, communicators, engineers, and leaders. We are all cross-trained in everything while individually specializing in certain talents.

SEAL Ops in the 1990s

During Vietnam and, to an extent, the Persian Gulf, we deployed to an area and were told "Get to work, start conducting SEAL operations." We were pretty much left alone (unless somebody thought we were doing something stupid) to generate our own missions.

That's completely changed. Now, we essentially stand by here in the United States or some forward base, waiting for something to happen and a specific tasking from a higher headquarters. When it does, we hop on an airplane or a boat and dash off somewhere to do the op. We wait to be told what to do, often by people who don't quite understand how to use us. When Ray Smith was running the show for us during Desert Storm, he'd get direction from the CINC–General Schwartzkopf and his staff–via the SOC (Special Operations Command). Ray would get a message saying, in effect, "We want you to go to these specific locations and conduct these specific kinds of missions." That is a lot more specific tasking than was once the case.

Now, that kind of control could have created terrible problems in Vietnam, but now we have a resource that helps make that kind quick-reaction operation possible: superb intelligence from overhead sources (photo-recon and electronic warfare aircraft, plus satellite photography). That is a big plus. It is counteracted by a big minus–our deteriorating capability to do "human intelligence," the information you get from talking to the local population in their own language.

Asking for Permission is Asking for Trouble

This "remote control" doesn't stop with the initial mission tasking; it continues throughout the whole op–if you don't turn off the radio. For example, I must now receive the mission tasking and the intel from above; that goes into a package, and we develop a *concept of the operation* to often include several *courses of action* (COAs). That concept goes back to my boss (and his boss) for his approval. Then I have to work up the concept in detail–and send that back for approval again! My boss will consider it, modify it, allocate some or maybe all the assets you asked for, then approve–or disapprove that modified plan.

Finally, you get to develop a tactical plan that you can use to brief the people going on the op. They've been milling around, trying to get organized for something . . . without knowing what will actually get approved. This is the kind of situation that caused big problems in Panama–people outside the organization, controlling the op, who weren't really in control. Then we have to ask permission, and that's asking for trouble. After all that you still have to brief the senior commander. He can approve or disapprove your "brief-back."

Asset Allocation

It used to be that the boat drivers lived alongside us. When we were getting ready for an op we'd go over and say, "Hey, we're going on a mission tomorrow night; you guys gonna be ready?"

Now, all assets are coordinated in a joint arena, with all the armed forces involved. If I need a boat in this brave new world, even one NSW already owns, I have to go to higher headquarters and ask permission–since somebody from another unit or even service may want to use it, too–then I must make a formal request for the boat, even though the skipper might be in the bunk next to mine. If I need a helicopter, owned by the Army or the Air Force, I might have to go way up the chain of command just to see if it is possible, then pull them into my planning before I get to use the helicopter. That makes the planning cycle far more complex, and complexity is also asking for trouble.

The complexity is offset, though, by wonderful helicopters and boats and radios. We have a much better capability in all our mobility platforms to get where we're going than ever before.

It used to be, in the Vietnam era, that you had a personal relationship with the helo pilots and the boat drivers; they lived and worked with you every day. I knew that if I got in trouble I could count on my friend Fred or Jack to come in and get me; today I probably don't know the helo pilots who can come from almost anywhere. If something goes to pieces today, will these guys who don't know me have the same kind of commitment as the guys who used to drink with me in the club? Probably not. So we plan that into the operation, too, with secondary and tertiary extraction and emergency plans.

Commo Follies

Once I get into the field I have better radio communications than ever before. This is not always a good thing! Better radios mean that, if I have a problem out there on an op, I can call for help much more reliably. It also means, unfortunately, if my boss, or his boss, or somebody way up there wants to call me and tell me what to do, they have that option as well.

When I am out on an op I really don't want people calling up with overly helpful advice and suggestions; that happened only twice on all my operations in Vietnam. I didn't like it either time–and in one case, the radio "malfunctioned" during the transmission receipt, and I could get away with shutting the PRC-25 off. That doesn't work well today, and I might have to take the direction whether I like it or not.

In Vietnam I could talk to the boat and the boat could talk to me–as long as we were within 3mi of each other. During the Gulf War, Ray Smith in the Gulf was able to call RADM George Worthington back here in Coronado on a daily basis if he wanted, just using our little satellite communications radio. Now, if the National Command Authority really wants to chat with me while I am out there on an op somewhere, they can do it. This, also, is not necessarily a good thing.

In fact, it isn't a good thing; I think the guy on the ground should always be the one calling the shots. He shouldn't get anything from the folks back at the ranch except support when he calls and asks for it. Once you've built a plan and gotten it approved, once you've been launched on a mission and things start to go wrong, you're the guy who is in the best position to decide what to do. If somebody back at the ranch comes up with information that will help you–"Hey, we see a platoon of enemy troops 3mi away, moving toward your position"–great, give me a call with that sort of thing anytime! But don't call up and say, "We want you to move three klicks to your left; there is a threat moving your way." Let *me* make the decision about how to react. But good communications has taken some of that command responsibility away from the SEAL mission leader. That's exactly how we got into trouble in the Iranian hostage rescue mission, with Jimmy Carter standing in the White House calling up Col. Beckwith, telling him what to do and micro-managing the operation. I don't like that; most of us in the SEALs don't like that. Some of us put up with it–and some of us say "Sorry, I can't read you–must be something wrong with the radio–OUT!"

There is something almost insidious about this improvement in communications. Some in the SEAL community are willing to let the responsibility slip upwards. There is a tendency to say, "okay, if they want to take responsibility for the op, fine, let them." The problem for me is, I still have a responsibility downward, to the men who are with me. When their lives, and mine, are hanging out there I don't want somebody far away making the calls that might get us all killed. And we've had a lot of SEALs killed just that way in the years since we learned our lessons in Vietnam.

The Fear Factor

SEALs have a world-wide reputation for being fearless warriors, masters of combat in a maritime environment. Well, we are premiere warriors in that element all right, but we certainly aren't fearless. It is something that builds up in you, normally while you are required to wait for some genuinely dangerous thing to happen. While we are waiting in the submarine's lockout chamber, or going in to shore in a Combat Rubber Raiding Craft (CRRC), or moving up a river for an insertion, there is almost always a lot of time to sit and think about what you're doing, and I think most of us have to deal with some genuine fear. It isn't something we encounter in training, no matter how realistic, but it is something that ought to be more important to our planning than it is. Fear is a factor in every SEAL mission, a factor that almost always has a significant effect on the op.

Fear isn't often an overriding factor in training because training is designed to be safe. When we train for patrol ops and somebody is clumsy and does something that would compromise the mission, nobody fires bullets at the patrol members, the way it happens on a real-world op. When we do subsurface swim training, nobody throws grenades in the water where the swimmers are, the way it happens in real life. We like to say that we train the way we fight–but that's not true. If we did we'd have to get people killed occasionally, for the sake of realism, and even SEALs don't advocate that.

So we do the best we can to prepare the trainees for what they will experience in combat. We are able, though, to put them under so much stress and make them so tired that they will begin to experience a little of the feeling of combat. There is some danger inherent even in our training: the parachute jumps, closed-circuit diving, the use of explosives, the way we practice for close-quarter combat by shooting near each other, all these things are somewhat dangerous. But until the guy next to you is shredded in an ambush you will probably feel pretty much invincible; then, quite suddenly, you will probably feel extremely vulnerable. And, even so, we need to have you overcome that and continue with your mission.

You'd think an outfit like the SEALs would be loaded with people with combat experience, who could pass along the lessons learned from real shooting matches to the new kids, but that's not the way it is right now. Although we have picked up some lessons from recent operations, when I left SEAL Team Three only five guys out of 205 on the team had any combat time at all! And of those five, not all had seen anybody get hurt.

So of the 205 guys on the team, only five really understand what it is all about. The rest may be thinking, "boy, this is fun, I really enjoy all this stuff." It can seem like playing war to some people. But back when we were sending over platoons of fourteen guys to Vietnam and often getting only ten guys back in one piece, everybody got their "head-space" adjusted real fast. A lot of guys who had been in the teams, enjoying the jumping, the diving, the shooting, and the rest of the training suddenly said "ah, I think I'd like to get out of this business. It doesn't seem like much fun anymore; see ya!" They got out of the Navy and we had to get along without them.

Bud-man's Silver Star

But you never know how a guy is going to behave under stress. We had one guy who started drinking a lot, so much so that we started calling him "Bud-man" for his favorite brand. When he drank he tended to bad-mouth everybody on the platoon. We couldn't have that, so we sent him home. He came back right away, though, with another platoon.

LT Mike Collins, an experienced SEAL veteran, commanded that platoon, with CPO Bomar as the 2IC (second in command). For the 2IC to be other than an officer was almost unheard of, but Bomar was good enough to rate this assignment. Bomar was a huge, brilliant, super-aggressive operator–6ft 5in and 280lbs of muscle. Within the first few months this platoon had over 100 percent casualties; everybody had been either killed or wounded. My heroic young petty officer, P. K. Barnes, was transferred to that platoon as we rotated out as a member of this platoon and lost his leg on one of its operations. Collins was killed, and so was Bomar. And this was home for "Bud-man," our reject. But when Bomar led a patrol into an ambush, got shot and lay dying on the beach with an arterial leg wound as the team was getting forced into the water, it was "Bud-man" who went back. The team had retreated across a canal under fire; "Bud-man" jumped in the water, swam the canal under fire, and retrieved the dying patrol leader. He got the Silver Star for that. And we quickly forgave him some of the nasty things he said about us when he was drunk.

Locking Out–The Chamber of Horrors

One of our most secure methods of insertion is also one of the most difficult and dangerous, the submarine lock-out procedure. Just to give you an idea of how complicated, dangerous, and demanding our ops are, let me brief you on it.

The sub comes in fairly close to shore–not so close that it

risks grounding or detection by enemy patrols, but a couple of miles off shore. Since it is extremely easy to see a submarine at the shallow depths necessary for this op, we try to only do this at night. The sub comes up to a depth of about 40ft; then a couple of divers lock out and set the stage for a boatload of SEALs to follow.

The divers climb into the sub's tiny escape chamber, a little compartment that permits a few people to exit the sub. The cycle for this process is slow and complicated. Once this first element exits they extract the collapsed boat and buoy from the locker where they are stowed, inflate the buoy, and send it to the surface on a line. The boat is inflated and rigged to this line so that it is riding on this tow line. When it is all safe and sound, the divers signal the sub that the boat is ready for the SEAL squad. This takes at least half an hour.

Now it is time for the squad to go. They climb into the chamber with their weapons and gear; since it is small, only three or four will fit during each cycle. Each is doubled over, weighted down with air tanks, and holding an armload of gear. Somebody has to squirm around and reach the flood valve, open it, and start the flooding process. Sound like fun? Nobody likes it, and I have personally seen guys actually panic in the chamber.

Once the chamber is full of operators, the hatches secured, and everybody has something to breathe, the chamber is flooded. When flooding is complete and the water pressure is equalized to the outside pressure, the exterior hatch is popped and everybody struggles out and up the line to the surface. While we normally use SCUBA tanks in the chamber and for the ascent, we sometimes use umbilical air lines in the chamber, then just hold our breath (of course releasing air going up) for a free ascent swim to the surface; we call this "blow and go." While it is pretty convenient for going up, it is more difficult when you are ready to come back aboard and have to swim back down 40ft or more.

If you're going to send out a full boatload of seven guys, this process takes at least two full cycles. While the second cycle is being brought up, the first three or four guys are sitting on the surface in the boat. Since it is out on the open ocean at night, and the wind is probably blowing, and all are soaking wet, they are freezing. Hypothermia and seasickness begin to degrade the capability of these people quite quickly. Since even the little rubber boat is a radar reflector, the submarine skipper will be extremely anxious; your boat marks his position as a target. As soon as everybody is up and aboard, the boat cuts loose, and the sub goes off on his business, and the boat crew moves off on their own.

Living Within the Schedule

Timing, as they say, is everything in this business. It is absolutely essential that everybody keep their activities within the schedule allotted to them. We do that in training; sometimes it happens in combat, but not often with the kind of quick, ad hoc missions we did in Panama and seem to be doing frequently. For example, my friend and business partner Norm Carley, got tapped to take Manuel Noriega's patrol boats out of the game plan at the beginning of Operation JUST CAUSE (the invasion of Panama in 1989).

The mission called for two swim pairs to be inserted out in the middle of the harbor by CRRC, swim in underwater, plant charges on the boats with time fuses, swim back out, and get picked up. Simple op, right? A nightmare op in the real world, even though they pulled it off.

For starters, the time for the kickoff got moved up while the planning was still in progress. When that happens everybody is already late. When you're late for a blind date like this, your adrenaline ratchets up a notch right away.

Then the motor for one of the two CRRCs malfunctioned. You'd think, with all the time we spend with CRRCs and small boat motors, that we wouldn't have reliability problems there, but the very slow speed needed for the insertion managed to foul the plugs on one engine and it wouldn't go. So there they were, out in the middle of Balboa Harbor, with boat traffic cruising past and a war about to begin. And a boat engine won't run–what would that do to your adrenaline level? But Norm, who not only commanded the op but did so from one of the CRRCs, has been around the block before; he'd been through the fear before and knew how to drive on with the mission. So the one boat that still worked towed the one that didn't, and they made the insertion pretty much on time.

When the swimmers arrived at the target ship and surfaced a firefight was in progress nearby. They didn't know if the CRRCs were involved, if they'd been detected; but they did know they had a job to do and a timeline. They got the charges placed and the timers started. But because of the firefight they had got trapped under the pier. The charges fired, shooting the ship's engine into space. The firefight in the vicinity slacked off, especially from Panamanian sailors on the target vessel. The swim pair got back in the water and swam back out to the extraction site, not really sure if the balky CRRCs would be there to meet them, but they were. In training we pull these things off with scheduled precision; in the real world, without a lot of real-world practice, they are often full of glitches and are often late.

I've discussed the difference between training and combat, and the fear factor, previously. Norm's mission illustrates some typical things that happen in the real world that don't happen in training. Norm and his team were under extreme pressure, and the adrenaline was really pumping; the Draeger closed-circuit re-breathers that ordinarily are good for 3-1/2-4hr in training burned out in about half that time. The fear factor changed the oxygen consumption rate for the swimmers and took it right off the scale we had worked hard to develop.

CHAPTER 3

Ethics and Morality

As everybody knows, the SEALs are a combat organization, a military organization that has done a lot of tough missions over the years in support of the national security interests of the United States. Well, everybody knows that in theory, but the dark side of our business is sometimes forgotten or ignored by people within our own organization. It is easy, during the long intervals of peace, to see all the training as a kind of enjoyable adventure. The parachute jumps, the diving, the shooting, the submarine ops, and the patrol exercises can be fun, a kind of game. We spend a lot of time in Hawaii, in the Caribbean, and on the beach at Coronado. We get good tans and plenty of opportunity to work out. SEALs know that we belong to a group that inspires awe in many people–you can pick up a girl in a bar a lot easier when she finds out you are a US Navy SEAL. So it is easy to slip into a kind of mind-set, as an individual, that overlooks and ignores the possibility that sooner or later some of us will have to load the weapons with live ammunition instead of blanks and shoot at targets that are living human beings instead of cardboard and paper–or worse, be shot at by "real" bullets. Does this seem too obvious? It is a recurrent problem for leaders at all levels of our business and one that I have struggled with over the years. I have had to do my best to shoot people, and when you shoot people you have to live with the decision, with the moral issues of killing, and with yourself.

One of our historically most common missions has been the ambush. It is a sneaky, bloody, dangerous business. SEALs have killed many hundreds of VC and NVA by hiding in the weeds and waiting for them to amble up the trail or paddle down the canal; then we machine-gun them. This is not a business for everybody–even though the training for it can (if you don't think about it too much) seem like fun. And it effects people in a whole range of different ways. One of those ways is that, when the shooting is about to start, a lot of your team mates suddenly decide they want to get out of the Navy and sell used cars or insurance.

Others stay and sometimes surprise you. One friend of mine refuses to fish or hunt with me; Steve will not hurt an animal of any kind, spiders included. When I go spear fishing, he goes along but won't take any fish; and he won't clean the fish afterwards because he's afraid the knife will inflict pain on the fish.

If you had to guess, wouldn't you expect someone like that to have a revulsion about taking human life, too? Well, my friend is absolutely fearless in combat. He has come face to face with enemy on the battlefield and stood toe to toe with them, shooting until he killed them. He has no problem whatever killing human beings, though, when it is part of his mission. This is an interesting ethical and moral conflict. And that friend isn't the only one.

Psychologists sometimes are called in to poke around inside our intellects to see how we tick. One interviewed my friend and posed this hypothetical question to him: "The United States has identified someone in a foreign nation as a dangerous individual. How would you feel about going after that individual and killing him?"

"Not a problem. When do I leave?" Steve replied.

"You wouldn't do that, would you?" asked the shrink, apparently appalled. "You wouldn't assassinate someone in cold blood?"

"If this guy is properly identified by my American chain of command as a legitimate target, I have no problem with it at all. That is part of our job and our responsibility." So said my friend Steve–the guy who won't go hunting or fishing because he doesn't like to hurt animals.

It being the 90's, we hear a lot abut the importance of guys being *sensitive* and *caring*. Well, the rumor is that SEALs are sensitive and caring type guys also. The difference, according to my good friend, Norm Carley, is that SEALs are *sensitive* to the needs of others and could *care* less. However, an incident that occured to me during my Vietnam tour in 1970 might portray this "tougher than thou" attitude in a different light.

My boss over there was reading the new hot novel which had come out and was sent to him by his wife. For those who were alive and reading back then, it was the extremely emotional romance called *Love Story*. I happened to walk in on my boss just as he was finishing the last few pages and caught tears in his eyes. I became so intimadated to read that book after seeing his reaction that eventually I decided to become a "closet reader" of that novel so that when the end of the book came, I wouldn't have anybody around to catch my reaction–just in case.

Onward Christian Sailors

During the time I commanded SEAL Team Three a senior chief, known to be very religious, worked for me as assistant operations officer. He was a great leader and motivator, a terrific guy to have in the unit, a self-starter who ran the Operations Shop with a firm, fair hand. This chief had an unusual knack for taking the initiative and confronting people who weren't doing things right, a leadership quality I think is especially valuable–and in short supply. I liked having him around. But as I got to know more about him, it turned out that he was a lay leader in his church. He spent a lot of time in bible study and was very religious.

As his commander I had an opportunity to make a career decision for him; he was up for an assignment which would culminate in his being a command master chief, but I really wasn't convinced that his religious training and convictions wouldn't conflict with our military missions. Certainly such convictions and Christian moral precepts have caused a lot of anguish for people in our profession in the past. While the chief was great in training, he'd never been on an actual combat operation, never been in Vietnam, never had to actually shoot at anybody. So I called him in and asked him about the problem.

"I know you have extremely strong religious convictions," I told him, "and that makes me wonder if you really belong in an organization like this one, considering the things we have to do. As long as we're sitting here in the US, in an administrative situation, you're a great leader. But there's no moral conflict with what we're doing here today. What if, next week, we get sent overseas; what if you and I have to conduct an operation that involves killing people? I know how you feel about your faith; how can you resolve that faith with this role?"

"Well sir," he said, "it is true that I am very religious. I take my teachings seriously and apply them to daily life. But when I come aboard this organization for duty, have no doubt that when the time comes I will be there and I will do what you need me to do."

He got the assignment; I had to take him at his word. But I still wonder how he could possibly reconcile the conflicts of the mission and the morals he professed. There is a moral conflict there, and I always wondered if he would be a trigger-puller out in the real world when the situation isn't a "self-defense" matter.

Up Close and Personal

It is this kind of "in your face" killing that separates all of us in the SpecOps community from the rest of the armed forces. The Air Force killed many Iraqis, soldiers, and civilians during the war in the Persian Gulf, but from a distance that made the experience remote and impersonal–for the aircrew who were launching the weapons, at least. The Army's tanks and artillery engage "targets" at ranges so long that you can't see them with the unaided eye; but when an M1 Abrams tank fires at an Iraqi T62, as many did, four human beings die an awful, fiery death. Our Navy's submarines and carrier air wings can deliver weapons at targets far away, out of sight. But SEALs and Green Berets and Rangers don't have that luxury; we have to confront our enemy's humanity in the age-old way. It can be hard.

Generally, it is a lot easier for me to (for example) use a mortar against a target off in the distance, out of sight, than to take a sniper rifle and line up on an individual enemy soldier and shoot him. The mortar prevents me from looking that man in the eye; I might respect and even admire that individual soldier–he might be a soldier just like me, an honorable and professional warrior, but on the opposite side.

On the other hand, I and most of us in this business, have no moral conflicts whatever about killing people we know to be genuinely evil; drug dealers and rapists in particular would fall into this category. But what do you do when you're executing a ship take-down and you encounter a crewman ready to surrender? You have to keep moving. You maybe can't take him prisoner, you maybe can't leave him as a threat; you may have to shoot him. SEALs have had to do this.

So Gary Gallager, my master chief at SEAL Team Three, and I used to go over to talk to the guys about to start Hell Week at BUD/S. Basically, what I told them was:

"Listen, guys, this is not a fun business. If you're thinking that after you get done here you will spend a career lifting weights, running on the beach in front of the girls, you are sadly mistaken. You are trying to get into a really tough business. Once you get through this training–if you do–you may be asked to go do some things that can be very difficult and very unpleasant. You or your friends might not come home from these assignments; you may be injured and disabled for life. If you have any doubts about your ability to complete these missions, don't put yourself through the rest of this most difficult of training. Don't waste our time if you aren't able to follow through."

CHAPTER 4

Leadership and NSW

We have a leadership problem in NSW today that we haven't had before, a serious problem that I have discussed with my community. We have young officers come into our organization who are highly motivated, the cream of the crop of new American naval officers. They want nothing more than to lead SEALs, and we train a few of the very best new ensigns to do this job; by the time they're trained they are lieutenants junior-grade. They get one or two solid deployments where they actually get to lead troops; once they've had a shot at leading a platoon of SEALs we jerk them out of the water and send each off to a staff job or a development program or to become a detailer back in the Washington DC area.

As soon as our junior officers finish their hitch with a platoon as a platoon commander, they are typically out of the field forever. We have many senior officers in the SEALs who have never experienced combat. They are completely out of touch with the experience of real-world operations. And yet they provide command and control of those operations and determine how to train for them. What's wrong with this picture?

The Navy's aviation community grows its leaders up through the ranks while keeping them proficient in flying skills; when we were in the Persian Gulf I had an admiral whom I had the highest respect for, Tony Less. He was the senior guy out there, in charge of the Joint Task Force, Middle East. One night, he came out to my barge to fly a night helicopter operation in support of me–and he's a jet fighter pilot! Here's a senior leader who still knows what it feels like to operate. We don't do that in NSW.

Our weapon system is the Mk 1 Mod 0 SEAL–a human

being who needs to be commanded by a leader who understands the total mission. When Norm Carley and I were doing combat ops in the Gulf we both received criticism for accompanying the troops on missions. We were told that the commander should stay well back, out of the action. Well, the Israeli commanders have a pretty good record in war, and they lead from the front; you'll find their combat leaders in the first tank crossing the "line of departure." My position is that the mission leader can sometimes lead best when he goes along on the op. Norm did it in Panama, and his presence and leadership probably had a lot to do with the success of his ship attack. When a SEAL Team leader goes along on a platform- or a ship-takedown op, he can still let the young lieutenants, the platoon leaders, command their units–but he can command and control those elements best when he, as the senior leader, knows what is really happening without delay or interpretation. When we, the senior tactical commanders, go down on the deck with the assault elements in harm's way along with everybody else, the maneuver elements get the best possible leadership, command, and control. But I will bet that less than ten senior officers in all of NSW have the experience–and courage–to actually participate on an op, to lead from the front.

Political Correctness and BUD/S

We are constantly pressured by both the Navy and the civilian agencies of government to turn BUD/S into a kinder, gentler experience. We take tremendous heat for the injuries and the high failure rate. Even SOC, our higher joint headquarters, has on occasion suggested we lighten up.

Well, we graduate an average of around 30 percent of the men who begin the training. We even had a class where NOBODY graduated! It is a hard program for a hard job. We are famous for having the worst success ratio in the armed forces, and we're constantly pressured to bring that ratio up.

We've tried numerous times to find the characteristics that predict success in BUD/S, so we could weed out the unlikely candidates in advance. We have studied, surveyed, run computer models, and spent large sums to find a reliable predictor of success; there isn't any. We looked at physical size, swimming ability, boxing experience–we couldn't find a clue. You'd think the big linebacker kind of guy would do well, and sometimes they do, but most of the guys who make it through BUD/S are of medium size and build. If there is a common quality, the only significant one seems to be a lack of skeletal or heart problems.

Despite the political pressures, I think we need to keep things the way they are. We've been doing this for fifty years. We found a system that turns out a man who is very successful on the battlefield. People want us to fix something that isn't broken–a notorious way of breaking something that works. We should never dilute or shorten the program, and we should just accept whatever success rate the system produces. We need to concentrate on the quality of the guy who makes it through, not the statistics.

Affirmative Action and NSW

One of the other things that drives the higher headquarters goofy is a remarkable lack of minorities and a total lack of women in SEALs. We have very few minorities in NSW and extremely few blacks in particular. Compared to the rest of the Navy or the population in general, we are way off the chart statistically at somewhere between 3 and 7 percent minorities in the organization at any one time. The Army has the same problem with Special Forces, and there are several apparent reasons.

Many black men, about 40 percent, seem to be "negatively buoyant;" that means they tend to sink rather than float. The reason we hear is a higher bone or muscle density. While it might seem unlikely, if you ever watch a qualification "swim test" you'll see what they're talking about; the black sailors (and black soldiers who want to be Green Berets) frequently struggle and sink and fail. Very few can pass the entry test. It is sad, unfortunate, and somewhat amazing to watch. And if you think this is the result of some hidden prejudice among the military, think of how many black Olympic swimmers you've seen. We get about the same ratio of black to white as you'll find on the average college swim team–and that's pretty low.

One other reason may be that the blacks who come to us typically come from communities where swimming and water sports are not traditional. That makes our primary activity something new and unfamiliar to many minorities who wish to join the SEALs.

Since the numbers are so low we are under pressure to let marginal minority BUD/S students slide just a little. Once aboard these marginal people are allowed to slide a bit more. That's wrong, and is a problem. We have some terrific minority SEALs but we also have a tendency to keep people who would be out the door if they weren't part of a protected class. During my active duty years we received direction from senior Navy staff to increase the numbers of minorities, especially blacks, no matter how we did it. That is wrong, for the individuals and for the organization.

What to do about it? We can't do anything about the bone density problem but we can encourage minority kids to start thinking about us at an earlier age, to get interested in water sports and to become familiar with the SEAL environment. South Africa has been quite successful with a program of mentoring black recruits, bringing them up to speed, and turning them into good, professional soldiers and sailors. We might be able to do something similar, but it would need to start at an early age, at the high school level or before, to be successful for

NSW. I would like to see something similar to a Junior Reserve Officers Training Course (JROTC) program instituted for SEALs; if these kids were introduced to the water early and learned to be comfortable in it, before they show up at our pool for the swim test, I think a lot of them would do just fine. This idea has been floated by senior Navy SEAL reservist CAPT Dick Couch.

Women and NSW

This is a touchy subject in NSW, and a radical attitude on my part, but I think there is a place for women in NSW, and it *isn't* in the galley. Without getting into the details, I can say that there are already women in certain special operations units. They are valuable and respected members of their units, highly qualified, and aggressively recruited. But they aren't SEALs or Green Berets or Army Rangers, for a variety of reasons.

While I think there's a role for women in our business, there is no place for women on the teams. Perhaps there are some females who could get through BUD/S but I don't think they'd be very recognizable as women. There are simply physical performance differences between men and women that are recognized and generally accepted; we have separate events at the Olympics for men and women, separate world records for marathon times and the 100 meter dash. Women certainly can stand pain and cold and do many things we require well. So can many men, but our standards keep them out, too.

I know women are often terrific divers. I teach and certify many of them in SCUBA and they are typically better than the male students–they listen better, do what they are taught, tolerate the cold, and make good divers. But that's very little of what it takes to being a SEAL.

Take these same women and put them in a set of greens, point them at the O course, and tell them to get over the cargo net or the Slide for Life, then put fins on them and throw them in the water for an hour and a half, then have them put a boat on their head and hold it for a while . . . they just can't do it. How do we know? Because we have tested women and done studies and trials and experiments. The physical differences in men and women, of equivalent age and at the peak of physical performance, are actually amazing–and well documented in reports and testimony before the Presidential Commission on the Assignment of Women In the Armed Forces in September 1992. With statistically insignificant exceptions, virtually no women can do the kinds of things we demand of the men. And we have taken a careful look at our tests, training, and missions to insure our standards made sense, relative to the real world, and for our special little world, the standards are, if anything, a little low.

The politicians in and out of the Navy don't seem to care about missions, though they want racial and gender equity, no matter what. The result is pressure to lower our standards. Pat Schroeder, a member of Congress from Colorado, has been a leader in this campaign; she appears to not understand or even really care about the real-world missions of SEALs but is only concerned that women are included in what she perceives as an elite unit. That might be a good tactic to get elected, but it is a poor tactic to develop combat units that successfully execute elite wartime missions.

While we don't have any operational women in the teams or, as far as I know, in NSW right now, I have been on covert ops by non-Navy units where women were part of the operation. These women did very well, and the ops couldn't have been done without their participation. And that's all I can tell you about it.

Getting Your Ticket Punched

We have another critical leadership problem in NSW, the

"ticket-punch" syndrome. At first our community was a place where people who really wanted to be warriors signed up. You might not get a lot of decorations or rank, but if you wanted to be an operator, the old UDT units and the later SEAL teams were the spot for you.

Then we got fashionable. We got a reputation. Sometime, in the ebb and flow of politics, NSW got lots of funding and support from both the Navy and the civilian component of government. Suddenly, about ten years ago, we started getting a lot of promotion slots. That attracted people whose idea of a successful career was measured in their individual rank progression rather than their contribution to national defense. These officers, and there are many in NSW, are primarily interested in all the awards and "ticket punches" that will help make them promotable. They see membership in the SEALs as a component of a strategy to attain a star. And they find lots of relatively safe, comfortable ways to move up the ladder. While the operators in the community know who they are, there are enough ticket-punchers already at high levels of command in SPECWARCOM that their breed is self-perpetuating.

The first time I noticed this was in Vietnam where I actually encountered two people who decided to recommend each other for combat decorations for incidents that didn't happen. Later I saw whole platoons sent out on ops where five men would normally be used; the intention was that all participants would get a Bronze Star or similar award without too much risk. For example, during the very brief and comparatively low-risk operation in Panama, JUST CAUSE, more combat decorations were "earned" by SEALs than by all the platoons conducting ops in entire six-month periods in Vietnam! In fact some Army personnel attempted to decline or outright refused awards of combat decorations because they felt they hadn't been legitimately earned by traditional standards. During World War II,

Korea, and Vietnam you pretty much needed to do something heroic or "above and beyond" to get a Bronze Star from the SEALs or the Green Berets; a high level of risk was just part of the job description and certainly didn't earn you anything. But a Bronze Star or higher is a great ticket punch when it comes time for the promotion board, and there are still people in NSW who think that way. I think it is disgusting.

Fakes and Phonies

Another sad, disgusting practice that causes a lot of trouble for us in all the armed forces is a rather large number of people who claim to be either heroes or members of elite organizations. As Barbara Walters revealed in a 1995 television special, a lot of guys claim to be combat vets from the Vietnam era; they are sometimes quite active in veterans organizations, do public speaking, and generally claim to be something they never were or to have done something, usually heroic, that they never did. Lots of guys claim to be Green Berets, and some show up at annual events; the SEALs have a similar problem with guys who want to be admired. Inventing a story is a lot easier than getting through BUD/S, so they make up a story. They can be quite compelling and difficult to detect sometimes.

I've encountered the problem directly on several occasions. The first was in Vietnam when a couple of guys strolled into the hooch claiming to be SEALs. Both were wearing "tiger-stripe" pattern uniforms and walked into our little team bar. "Can we have a beer?" they asked. Bill Cheatham, the current commander of SEAL Team Five, was a petty officer, second class, at the time and a very hard-core guy; "Sure," he said, looking them over. The uniform didn't compute for Bill and he started a polite little interrogation session.

"How come you guys are wearing tiger-stripes?" Bill wanted to know.

"Oh, we've been over in Cambodia running some secret ops. We're just in for a little R&R."

"Really," Bill said. "Who are you assigned to?"

"We're with SEAL Team Seven," one answered.

"That's interesting. Do you know where you are right now?"

"No, not really."

"Well, you are currently sitting in the SEAL Team One Kilo Platoon hooch. There is no SEAL Team *Seven.* You guys are a pair of phonies . . . and I will give you both about ten seconds to get out of here." They put their drinks down and evaporated; we didn't see them again.

More recently I was up at a Navy installation at Adak, Alaska. A little stocky petty officer, first class, met me and introduced himself. He'd been a SEAL, got injured, and had to get a new line of work. But he introduced me to his boss, the base security officer, a man who both claimed to be a former member of the SEAL teams–and he claimed to have known me, too! We chatted for a few minutes and compared notes. He was in SEAL Team One, he said, back from 1968 to 1972. Well, I was there from '70 to '72, and I just couldn't place him.

"Whose platoon were you in?" I asked.

"Oh, I wasn't assigned to a platoon," he said, "I was working with MACV/SOG (Military Assistance Command, Vietnam/Special Operations Group) the whole time and was in and out of Vietnam all the time. That's probably why you don't remember me."

"Well, what BUD/S class were you in then?"

"Jeeze, sir, I just can't remember what that class number was," he said . . . and I immediately knew I was talking to a phony. You NEVER forget your class number! You know your BUD/S number as well as you know your social security number or your home address.

"Hmm," I said. "Master Chief Gallagher is coming in this afternoon; remember him?"

"Oh, sure," he said. "Of course I remember him!"

Gallagher showed up, and I briefed him on the problem: the base security officer was a security problem himself. We collected the installation's command master chief and went looking for our imitation SEAL, and we found him just as he was departing the base security office. Gallagher walked up to the guy and started to politely check up on the information I had just given. The guy claimed to have been in our team and claimed to have been deployed to MACV/SOG during the times our assignments should have overlapped.

"Gosh, that's *really* interesting," Gallagher said, "because *I* was working with MACV/SOG during that time, too! And I don't remember YOU! In fact, *you are a phony*–and you had better get that 'Budweiser' off your shirt in a hurry or I am going to take it off for you and put it where the sun doesn't shine!"

The security officer chief started to cry. He went back in his office, took the emblem off. His young assistant, who really had been a SEAL, wanted to know what was happening, and the chief had to admit the truth. But that wasn't the end of the story; the chief's records were investigated, and a couple of very dubious decorations were discovered. He had actually been a boat driver but had managed to manipulate his personnel file to look like a SEAL. He knew the names of many of us from being in the boats and was able to fabricate a convincing story.

Just in the last couple of years I have encountered people claiming to be or to having been SEALs who just didn't seem right; I have called the teams with names and social security numbers and in about half a dozen cases have had my suspicions confirmed–the guys were lying. In one case, an officer aboard a ship turned out to have not only never been a SEAL but didn't even actually have a commission!

Fred Francis and the Media Weenies

Most people know we don't like the news media very much. That attitude is usually attributed, especially by people in the media, to hostile news coverage during the war in Vietnam. Actually it wasn't that the coverage of the war was just hostile to the American armed forces because there were lots of legitimate things a reporter could criticize. Lots of us encountered so much dishonesty, physical and moral cowardice, and deceit among the American news media back then and since that we typically avoid everybody from the media as we would an enemy. In fact some journalists and reporters seem clearly sympathetic to our enemies and hostile toward us and our missions.

Others just don't care one way or another; they just want a good story. NBC's Pentagon Correspondent Fred Francis is a case in point. Our tanker escort mission during the Iran-Iraq War was a dangerous, difficult, and newsworthy event. But our barge and everything and everybody on it were super secret. No media was allowed anywhere near, much less aboard. Then I got a message: NBC was sending its military affairs corespondent, Fred Francis, and a camera crew to do a story on us–with the general's blessing!

I got on the phone to my boss. "Sir, nobody's supposed to be out here!"

"I know, Gary," he said, "but this seems to be some kind of payback for the secretary of defense for some favor he owes NBC for something they had done for him–or hadn't done to him. We have to do it. Just be real careful about what you say and what you let them film." So they came aboard.

As soon as they got off the helicopters and unloaded their crew and gear I knew this wasn't going to be fun. Nobody told me one of the cameramen was a *camerawoman*; we hadn't seen a woman in months! We also had no private facilities for a woman aboard the barge. But these were minor problems compared to dealing with Fred.

"I want to get some shots of the helicopters in flight," Fred said as soon as we started discussing what he wanted to cover.

"They don't fly in daylight," I told him, "and besides they are designated SECRET."

"Well, they are going to fly in daylight for ME," Fred said. "General Crist told me I could have anything I want out here, and I want to film those helicopters!" General Crist was our four-star US Marine Corps boss, then CINCCENT (Commander in Chief, Central Command) and predecessor to General Schwartzkopf.

"I'm going to send you up to my Communications Center where you can call him; just be sure to tell him that I said no." A young sailor was detailed to escort Francis to the Comm Center–while I made a dash for my own phone and called my admiral. "Stick to your guns" he told me. I did, and Fred lost Round One.

But he did get to watch the helos launch at night–and he didn't tell me that he had night vision lenses for the video cameras. His videotape of our helicopters, even taken at night, would reveal a lot to our adversaries. The Navy had to negotiate with NBC to censor that material, and it wasn't easy to keep it off the evening news.

Francis and his crew continually attempted to collect material they were told they couldn't get–the name of the barge, interviews with and names of the crew, all sorts of information that was supposed to be secret and that was going to stay secret as long as I had any control at all over the activities of these people on my vessel. We had to keep an "escort" on these people every minute, or they would have taped anything they could pull from our crew, regardless of what I had told them and without any concern for our mission or our personal safety.

CHAPTER 5

Weapons and Technology

One of the problems and issues confronting us in the SEAL community is a mind-set that comes from leaders whose experience has been as administrators rather than as operators. An example is the big debate about the proper pistol cartridge for SEALs and others in the special ops professions to use. Back in 1976 we set up the JSAAP (Joint Small Arms and Ammunition Program), a system to evaluate small arms and ammunition for all of us in the US Special Operations Forces. The idea was to do research and development, to come up with better weapons and better bullets. We always need weapons that shoot accurately, reliably, and when they hit, that kill better.

A great debate developed over the best pistol round: what's better, the 9mm or the .45cal? The Israelis came along and said, "None of the above–try the new, improved 10mm!" Then somebody came up with the .40cal; each has its passionate advocates and defenders in a long, loud discussion.

My reaction to this is, so what? We don't hunt with pistols, the issue is irrelevant! The pistol is a police weapon, not a special ops weapon, except in very unusual circumstances. This issue is being driven by a group of folks in the acquisition and procurement program who aren't operators and who don't think about how things work on the real-world battlefield. The proper weapon for our operations is the assault rifle, preferably the CAR-15 or M16 or Heckler and Koch (H&K) MP5, and not the pistol. Even so, we've spent millions of dollars on a wild-goose chase after the perfect cartridge for a weapon we won't (or shouldn't) fire.

All dressed up and nowhere to go. Members of SEAL Team One's Kilo Platoon ready for a night out in the jungle in 1970.

The temperature is about the same, but the plant life is sure not like that in the jungle. The author taking a break from Vietnam predeployment training out near the Salton Sea, next to El Centro, California, in 1970.

A prototype of the Mk XV Swimmer Life Support System, which was being tested for approval for service use in 1976.

The front door of Kilo Platoon's plush quarters near Rach Soi in Vietnam 1970.

A small security outpost manned by South Vietnamese on an island several miles offshore from Rach Gia in IV Corps.

The joint US/Vietnamese Navy riverine base located at Rach Soi, of which we were a tenant of during our deployment to Vietnam.

Our MSSC coming ashore on an island about 8mi offshore from Rach Soi to conduct an afternoon of R&R, away from the canals and operations.

Target practice across the expansive Cai Lon River coming out of the Delta just north of the infamous U Minh forest; the water was about 60ft deep most of the way across.

Kilo Platoon and its MST (Mobile Support Team) detachment outside their quarters on the riverine support base.

Nice surroundings, but some VC supply types were known to have been in a village just a short distance from here.

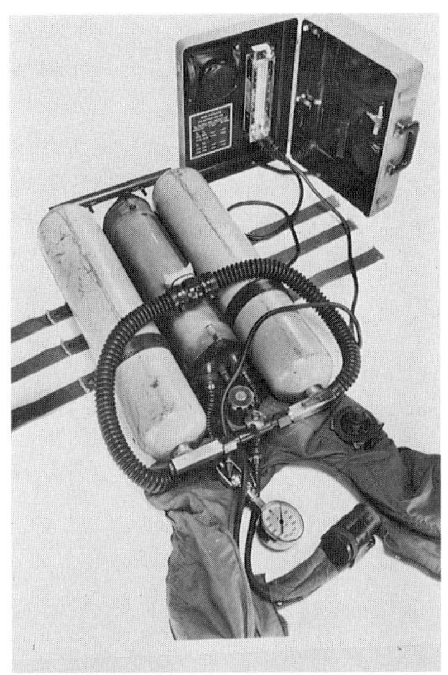

The old, no-longer-used MK VI mixed-gas unit used by the UDT frogmen when diving deep.

The type boat preferred by most SEALs and VC—the sampan. If we looked like one of them, sounded like one of them, and went where they went, they tended to think we were one of them.

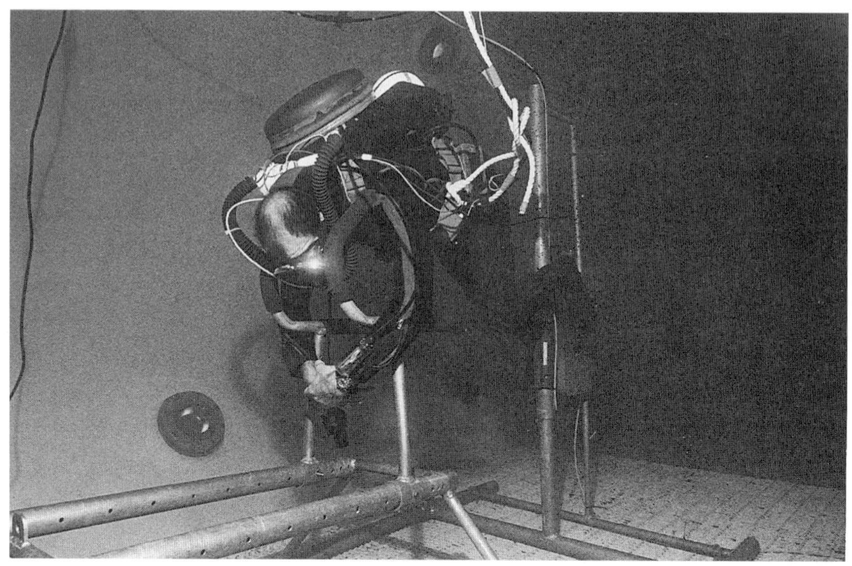

The author peddling as hard as possible for as long as possible, and still not getting anywhere. This was one of the ways the Experimental Diving Unit learned how long a new diving rig, in this case the prototype Mk XV, would last on a bottle of oxygen. It was the underwater version of the ergometer. In this instance, the pressure in the test tank was equivalent to the pressure under 165ft of seawater. US Navy

The Mk XV prototype being swum in the pool before being allowed to venture out into the open water. Part of the long, arduous means of safety and reliability testing that is part of development of every new piece of hardware.

Reconnaissance of a target "hooch" along the Cai Lon to determine the patrol route and where to insert by boat.

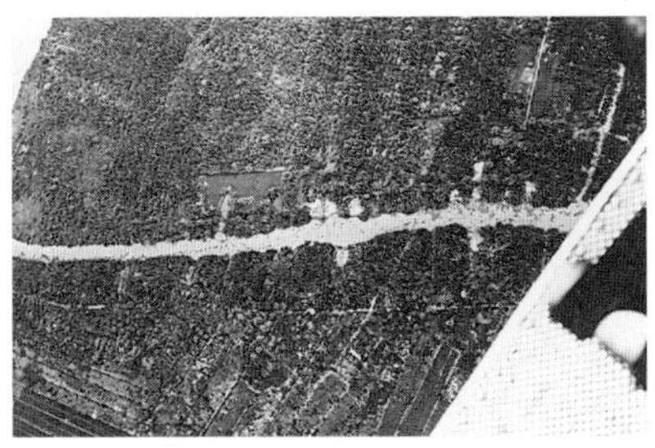

Locating a small tributary canal that feeds off the Cai Lon, which we can use to move further toward the target by sampan.

Bend in the Cai Lon. Note the triangular shaped security firebase near the center of the photo and beside a small tributary canal, with other canals moving off of it. Waterways in Vietnam's Delta are like side streets in our cities.

Creating fishing holes in the farmer's fields with 500lb bombs was a favorite pastime of the B-52 bomber crews. Note the four in this photo.

A view of our projected ambush site about a klick outside the village and at the intersection of the small canal coming in from the left to the main canal. The site provided plenty of concealment and the potential for various patrol routes in and out.

United States Navy SEALs going through the South Korean Marine Corps mountain warfare training course near Masan in the southern tip of the peninsula.

A footbridge over the canal near the riverine support base at Rach Soi that was used to connect the village along both sides of the canal.

A seabag layout for deployment during the early 1970s shows the relatively small amount of gear we needed for our operations in Vietnam. Today's load-out for an individual would take up over four times this area.

A photo of the fish traps crossing the Cai Lon where we met with the NVA unit that was crossing the river the same night we passed by in the MSSC en route to our insertion point for an ambush.

Top-notch US ammunition supplies. Note the condition of the .50 caliber linked ammo in the open ammo can. Much of what we received to fight with in Vietnam was in such poor condition as to be unusable.

This helicopter is trying to make the back of a small tug grow a helipad quickly. Extracting from a ship takedown training exercise in the Persian Gulf using a UH-60 helicopter flown by the US Army's Task Force 160 (the Nightstalkers) and caving ladders.

Another view of extraction from a ship takedown.

Our platoon pet that we found during one of our patrols. It entertained us by swallowing ducks whole until some Vietnamese decided our pet was big enough to eat for dinner.

A typical village along the friendly banks of a canal upon which we were transiting back from an overnight operation.

CWO Ron Fox pulling out of the Vietnamese riverine support base with the MSSC to test it before using it on an operation later that night. Note the Vietnamese PBRs in the background

The big barge Hercules in the northern Persian Gulf in 1988 as we were about to come in for a planning meeting and dinner.

The barge Wimbrown VII with our tow tug and a Mk III PB moored alongside. Note the two helo decks fore and aft. This, the smaller of the two barges being used by the SEALs in the northern Persian Gulf, was prohibited from having any more hardware placed on it because it was beginning to bend down on both ends from the excess weight and would be unstable if more pounds were added. In effect, we were told to put the barge on a diet.

A C-130 aircraft dropping a CRRC and jumpers out the back–known as a "rubber-duck" operation.

A rubber-duck operation about to end. The CRRC is being chased by the SEALs who will de-rig it upon reaching it in the water and begin their operation. It was an operation similar to this during which four SEALs were killed during the invasion on Grenada in 1983.

A flock of US-designed, Korean-built patrol boats in the harbor at Chinhae in the southern coast of the South Korea.

The town of Chinhae included the headquarters of the Korean Navy and the US Navy facility established to assist the Republic of Korea (ROK) Navy in its various programs.

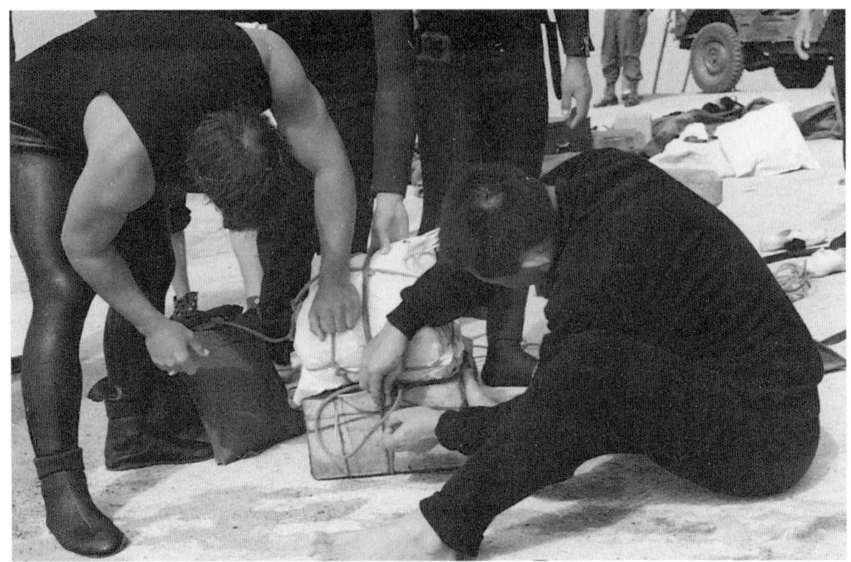

Getting ready for a joint US and ROK SEAL/UDT civic-action demolition project to use underwater demolitions to clear some navigational hazards in a fishing village on the southern island of Cheju Do, about 1974.

The results of the demolitions being initiated in the harbor off Cheju Do in the ROK. These projects provided excellent training for the US and Korean SEALs and frogmen, and at the same time were beneficial to the local fishing industry.

Larger ship traffic could transit through the Cheju Do harbor once the obstacles had been removed from the passageway.

A former World War II small, amphibious landing craft that had been provided to the Koreans during the Korean conflict. It was still providing amphibious support during training exercises during 1975 and beyond.

Mr. Ball, the Secretary of Navy and ADM Tony Less visiting the barge Wimbrown VII in the Persian Gulf during 1988.

Wimbrown VII–a mobile SEAL seabase in the Persian Gulf during the 1988 Iran-Iraq war. Note the Mk III PB alongside and helicopter platforms on each end of the barge.

Left
A UH-60 lifting off the forward helipad on Wimbrown VII. Note the Mk III PB in the cradle on the starboard side deck.

Below
The author (bald head) and his units fast-roping from a UH-60 (with a mini-gun sticking out of the gun port) onto a simulated target vessel during daytime practice for ship takedowns. Note the barge Hercules in the background.

The author and his command-and-control unit setting security and issuing directions to his four squads, who are moving through the simulated target vessel during daytime ship takedown training. The task becomes exponentially more difficult at night.

The families of the soldiers lived in the small outposts along the canals. This man was the officer in charge of this firebase just off the Cai Lon River in IV Corps.

ADM Tony Less conferring with CDR Norm Carley and CDR Gary Stubblefield during a visit by the Chairman of the Joint Chiefs of Staff, ADM William Crowe to the mobile seabase Wimbrown VII.

Gary Stubblefield Cdr.

A typical firebase along a canal set up to monitor traffic and hopefully deter the movement of VC personnel and supplies.

Then LTJG Tom "The Hulk" Richards, now RADM Richards, during a brief meeting in Bien Thuy during the period his platoon and Kilo Platoon were in Vietnam together. Note the relaxed grooming standards of the Zumwalt Navy era.

One of the mini-guns that we carried on our MSSC to help suppress fire when we encountered an ambush or persistent enemy along the banks of the canals. The mini-gun is still a formidable weapon today.

A beautiful pagoda located along a canal outside Rach Gia, not yet damaged by the war being waged around it.

Playing in the mud at the mud flats on the third day of Hell Week for Class

Looking north toward the Three Sisters from outside of Rach Gia. These mountains were loaded with VC and NVA troops. On every occasion to fly near them during helicopter recons, we received fire.

Can a prisoner of war get peaceful through osmosis? This detainee was being held at the Kilo platoon quarters awaiting transfer to the local holding facility for questioning.

Ready to go! During Vietnam, the equipment was kept ready for each member to throw on and get moving at a moment's notice. In those deployments, most of the platoon's equipment, both personal and unit, could be staged on two small airplane pallets. Nowadays, it takes at least ten pallets.

Looking down the Cai Lon toward the fish traps where we were ambushed when we encountered a company of NVA crossing the river the night before.

The author (with hair) and a fellow SEAL and the CO of the MST returning from conducting a reconnaissance up the river in preparation for a mission.

A watch tower at our riverine support base to try to spot VC setting up mortars or swimming down the river to carry out a swimmer attack against the patrol boats. We would hear concussion grenades going off at any given time to try to discourage the swimmers.

A US Navy Seawolf helicopter gunship belonging to the detachment assigned to Rach Gia

Two of our Kit Carson scouts with two of the rockets and a shaped charge captured during one of the raids on a VC logistics storage facility.

Well, actually, we do fire the pistol–many thousands of rounds a year per person–on the range, in practice. I love it, it's fun and relieves stress. But when I go hunting, unlike on television, I leave the pistol at home. So do the rest of SEALs. But we don't emphasize shooting our rifles nearly as much, even though that's what we fight with.

One of our lessons learned in Vietnam was that everybody needed to be extremely proficient with their rifles before going on operations. It was then common to give each guy 2,000 rounds for the M16 and then fire it all in a day! The team training cadre would tell us, "I don't care if your fingers start bleeding, keep loading and shooting until you can load magazines and shoot with one hand, in the dark!" We got to be really good shots under adverse combat conditions.

The origin of the current attitude, which I believe is misguided, has its roots in a real world situation that happened during Vietnam. One of our weapons specialists, RJ Thomas (now a retired commander), was out on a mission, and the helicopter he was riding in got shot down. One of the pilots was killed, and many aboard were injured. Then the VC started closing in. Thomas had no other weapon at the moment (though perhaps he should have been carrying a primary weapon) than a .45cal service pistol–with which he was extremely good. He used that pistol to hold off the VC. Ever since, the .45 pistol has been an object of cult worship for some in NSW.

My point is that, while the pistol may be a very handy weapon sometimes, we don't hunt with it as a matter of routine and we shouldn't put a lot of time and resources into something we are unlikely to use. We put a lot more time, energy, money, and imagination into working with the combat pistol than the rifle–the weapon we are more likely to use, and that's a mistake. As much as I like shooting a pistol for fun, when we were getting ready to do ship takedowns in the Gulf, I left the pistol in the weapons locker and worked with the CAR-15 every day, the weapon I wanted to carry on any operations.

The Weapon of Choice

We spend a lot of time trying to figure out what the best weapon for a SEAL is, and there isn't one. The best weapon is the one you know and are proficient with. That doesn't mean we can all use different weapons with different calibers. We need to be able to share ammunition, for example, or to pick up somebody else's weapon and use it effectively.

My personal bias is that the rifleman needs something between the M16 or CAR-15, the M-14, and the MP5 submachine gun; the long barreled version of the CAR-15 will accommodate the M203 grenade launcher, the MP5 is good for a short-range, close contact situation where maneuverability is important, and the M-14 gives you extra penetration power and extra range. Those are basic weapons considerations; the actual choice should be dictated by the mission rather than by personal preference. In some rare situations, it might be more prudent to carry an indigenous weapon such as the AK47 to look like and sound like the local bad guys. The most important factor is placing rounds where you want them!

The Rifleman

The riflemen on a patrol are supposed to engage "point" targets, and they ought to be firing single shots. The CAR-15s and M16s in use today have the choice of single shots or three-round-bursts; the old version could shoot full-auto. We learned in Vietnam that full-auto was almost always a mistake; we wasted ammo and didn't hit the target as effectively. Personally, I don't even believe in using the three-round-burst option.

The Machine-gunners

The M60s provide "area" fire that will keep the enemy's head down while we maneuver and engage. Automatic weapons provide cover for us, suppressing the enemy's fire and protecting ours.

Double-Tapping

You hear a lot of talk among combat shooters about "double-tapping" a target. The idea is to fire one carefully aimed shot at a target, followed immediately by a second aimed shot for insurance. I don't endorse this idea–if you hit where you aimed the first time, why bother? I teach people to watch what happens with the first shot, then fire again only if necessary. When we shoot in combat we need to engage our targets until we take care of them; that might be with one shot, or with many. But the shooter needs a certain amount of calmness and alertness to evaluate his shooting–conditions not always present in combat. I've never "double-tapped" a deer on a hunting trip. Here's an example from real life:

We were moving up on an insertion point aboard an LSSC, the engine at idle. Just before we were ready to go ashore, we suddenly got hit with automatic weapons fire from the shore; I said, "let's get out of here!" and the coxswain applied full throttle; nothing happened with the boat, though, because the jet pump inlets were clogged with weeds as so often happened with this particular craft. The whole boat opened up on the banks while we drifted for a few moments as the coxswain back-flushed the propulsion system.

It became apparent during this maneuver that the enemy fire was coming only from one side of the river. We brought the boat around to exit their "killing zone" and made a break for the exit. I had originally been on the side of the boat facing the enemy and I returned fire along with everybody else. But when we turned around and were facing the opposite bank I could see no enemy fire coming at us. There were no targets to engage in our fields of fire. I stopped shooting.

My second-class petty officer was still blazing away. He noticed me, watching but not shooting. "Sir–what's wrong? Why aren't you shooting?"

"There's nothing over here to shoot at," I told him. Only then did he notice that he had been on a kind of mental "full-auto." We all need to be calm enough under fire to evaluate our targets and our own performance.

An Even Break

SEALs don't march in, line up in neat rows, and pick a fair fight. Ideally, the enemy rarely knows we are present until the battle is basically over and won. SEALs sneak in, set up on the enemy, and unleash an overwhelming hail of gunfire onto the intended target before the target has a chance to react. We should not give them an even break. Unfortunately, there are a new generation of young team warriors that are beginning to think that we are supposed to play by the rules; that we should square off in the middle of the jungle trail like gunfighters or the duelers of the 18th century and whoever is the fastest or most accurate will be the winner. This is a good way to lose the duel. I have always felt that our business is safer than that of pilots or even ship drivers in a battle. We have a phenomenal amount of control over our destiny by planning and executing our missions. Its hard for the engineman in the engine room deep in the bowels of a surface combatant to effectively defend himself from an incoming missile. But we can plan our routes, type of mobility platform, where to insert, what firepower to use, and usually operate clandestinely enough to avoid contact except when we choose.

CHAPTER 6

A Short History of Frogmen and SEALs

The organization called the US Navy SEALs was born in the western Pacific Ocean over fifty years ago during World War II. One of our first real amphibious operations, the invasion of the Japanese island fortress of Tarawa by the US Marine Corps in 1943, produced a terrible disaster when the first assault waves became stranded well off the beach. Sand bars and reefs prevented the landing craft from going closer. The heavily-laden infantry tried to slog 500 yards through the surf just to get to the beach. Japanese machine-gunners swept the surf and the beaches with interlocking fires. There was no place to hide, no retreat, and the Marines died by platoons, companies, and battalions. It has been, ever since and forever more, *Terrible Tarawa* to every US Marine and sailor.

While there were plenty of lessons learned from Tarawa, the primary one was that amphibious assaults risk failure if the planners don't know for sure that they can get the troops to the beach. The people who had planned Tarawa assumed a normal beach gradient all the way to the high water mark; they guessed wrong, so thousands of Marines died. As a result the Navy quickly threw together a little unit of combat swimmers dedicated to mapping possible invasion beaches. It didn't take long for these swimmers to get another job, the touchy problem of clearing anti-invasion or natural obstacles with explosives. They were very special men with an extremely special mission; they were christened, at first the Scouts and Raiders, later, the Underwater Demolition Teams (UDT). Fifty years and more ago, they developed the art of combat swimming:

hydrographic reconnaissance, beach clearance, and the demolition of underwater obstacles.

Initially, these first-generation American "frogmen" didn't have masks, cold-water protection, or breathing supplies–they jumped into the often-frigid ocean wearing no more than swim trunks and splashed off on their missions. They learned to chart beaches with lead lines and slates from the protection of the water, and they learned how to sneak ashore to watch the enemy. SEALs still do much the same thing with the same slates, lead-lines, and grease-pencils today.

Although not part of UDT, there were other programs developed during World War II that also became part of today's US Navy SEALs; one was the Coast-watchers, a very small group of particularly brave men who lived ashore for long periods among the enemy, sending reports by radio on Japanese strength and activity. Although these men could hide themselves in the jungle or local terrain, every time they transmitted their radios they offered a beacon to the enemy, pinpointing the exact location of the coast-watcher. It took an exceptional man to execute this surveillance mission then–and it still does today. A good reference to this activity was *The Rice Paddy Navy* by Admiral Merry Miles.

By the end of World War II there were many underwater demolition teams–and they were mostly discarded, with their experience, their missions, and their fledgling equipment.

Korea

Just five years later, in 1950, the need for the UDT units surfaced again, in Korea. The US Navy had to reinvent this part of the amphibious wheel all over again but with the help of some veterans of earlier frogman days. This time the same beach survey and beach clearance missions were assigned, but some of the old coast-watcher missions were added, too, plus some experiments with excursions past the high-water mark and raids inland. This was the beginning of the kind of US Navy mission that we call today "special operations."

Combat swimmers charted the treacherous Inchon harbor, preparing the way for Gen. Douglas MacArthur's brilliant end-run amphibious assault. The Inchon harbor's tides, which ran around 20ft, were so treacherous and extreme that the North Koreans must have felt secure. But with good hydrographic recon provided by the UDTs, the US Navy put the US Marine Corps ashore to rout the North Koreans.

The UDTs expanded the role to more than just beach survey; they started actually doing the missions that had been discussed during World War II but not really tried–raids, assaults, and sabotage from the sea. They crawled up on enemy beaches and blew enemy radar sites, fortifications, and rail bridges.

We lost almost as many men in Korea as in Vietnam, but you seldom hear about them today. But that was the time and they were the men who started pulling together all the elements of the SEAL mission of today.

Almost as soon as the UDTs were back up to speed and mission effective, the Korean conflict was over, and the whole program was primarily shelved again. During the Cold War, with its huge investment in the idea of apocalyptic nuclear battles between massed Warsaw Pact forces and the forces of the North Atlantic Treaty Organization (NATO), the need for amphibious landings, much less the bravery of a few lunatic combat swimmers, seemed to most planners very slight indeed.

Well, so it seemed to *most* planners, but not quite all. One Naval combat veteran studied the threats to the United States and came to a different set of conclusions. That veteran was John F. Kennedy, elected president in 1960. Instead of nuclear exchanges by bombers, missiles, and submarines, Kennedy foresaw a kind of shadow warfare, often by surrogates, on the margins of NATO and the Warsaw Pact. Such conflicts were already in progress during the late 1950s and early 1960s, in Malaya, throughout Southeast Asia, in Cuba, Latin America, and elsewhere. For these conflicts, nuclear weapons were impotent.

Kennedy knew the British Army was defeating an insurgency in the jungles of Malaya through a combination of unconventional military and political tactics. The campaign was imaginative, innovative, and reminiscent of things that the US had tried successfully during World War II–by the Office of Strategic Services (OSS) in France and Asia, for example. When Kennedy came to power in February of 1961, he quickly demanded that the armed forces of the United States develop what came to be called an "unconventional" warfare capability. He found some of that capability already in place in the US Army–the little Special Forces outfit assembled by Col. Aaron Bank at Ft. Bragg, North Carolina.

Kennedy knew the Army leadership *loathed* this little congregation of outlaws. They represented everything the modern Army of 1961 was not–they fought with small arms and tiny units; they didn't wear starched uniforms and look good in parades; they cheated during war games (and won); and they wore that Goddammed green beret when they thought nobody was looking. Kennedy looked at these guys and said, in effect: *this is the new, action Army.* It was love at first sight.

The Navy and Air Force, along with the Army, were directed to develop and emphasize an unconventional warfare capability based on the "Green Beret" (although the term is common, it was invented by a journalist and is entirely unofficial) model. For the Navy, that was naturally based on the old, previously somewhat obsolete UDT frogmen. Some of these guys were trained in new skills such as parachuting, foreign languages, infantry and weapons tactics, plus some "nation-building" abilities such as building schools and treating civilians for disease and parasites.

The first SEAL teams-One and Two-were formed in 1962. The big problem was coming up with an acronym for the unit, but Sea/Air/Land seemed to work–nobody laughed too hard at it, anyway, so "SEAL" it was. SEAL Team One set up shop on the West Coast, at Coronado, California; SEAL Team Two on the East Coast at Little Creek in Norfolk, Virginia.

Each new SEAL team had ten officers and fifty enlisted sailors. The commanding officer (CO) of each was just a lieutenant. The structure of the team, naturally, was based on an Army infantry model with fire teams, squads, and platoons.

Deployments to Vietnam began in 1962. Until 1968 the role of these deployments was limited and involved a lot of training of Republic of Vietnam (RVN) naval units. SEALs did some direct action missions, and they taught Vietnamese sailors how to conduct coastal operations; then they went out with these students on missions to advise and sometimes lead. It was a process called "force-multiplication." It sometimes worked then, and it sometimes works today.

Force Multiplication–and Division

This is about the time I earned my flippers and became a SEAL. I'll tell you more about how I became a SEAL later, but my first personal experience with the real-world NSW community and its mission began in Vietnam and with this "force-multiplication" mission. I worked with the "Kit Carson scouts" and also did some work with a Vietnamese SEAL unit called the LDNN for *Lin Dai Nui Nai.*

The LDNN were members of the RVN navy, many of whom had been brought to the US and trained in SEAL tactics and techniques out at Niland, California, in the desert near the Salton Sea, who were then returned to be unleashed against the VC and NVA. While some of these guys were good, hard-charging fighters, most were not. The priority for many seemed to be to collect their pay every two weeks, have fun in Saigon at every opportunity, and to stay out of the line of fire. They weren't interested in operating, and they weren't loyal.

We did have some good people, mostly the Kit Carson scouts–enemy soldiers who'd changed sides or Cambodians that came down as sort of mercenaries. A lot of these guys turned out to be very effective. I had three of these guys assigned to me, plus one of the few good LDNN guys, Mr. Lac, to serve as an interpreter.

Early on, SEALs worked with another program, set up by the US Central Intelligence Agency (CIA) and highly classified at the time, called the PRU or Provincial Reconnaissance Units. The recruits for this little outfit were bandits, thieves, and assorted rabble recruited from Vietnamese jails. They were trained, equipped, and organized into small units of about thirty or forty, with one or more US Navy SEALs to provide baby-sitting services and training; the CIA then provided logistic support–weapons, food, clothing, payroll–plus command and control. Since these guys knew so much about the countryside they became quite good at sweeping up the loyal opposition. The PRU became quite adept at collecting enemy tax collectors, complete with receipts, and any other high value target, and the revenues from these excursions helped further fund and motivate the PRU. Of course our guys were removed administratively from their membership in the US Navy SEALs while working for "The Agency" (as it is called). The SEALs assigned to the PRU dressed in civilian clothes and had civilian cover stories, and their ID cards were stashed in somebody's office safe. Of these three programs, the PRU and Kit Carson scouts did good work, and the LDNN didn't, but that was just part of the learning curve for us all.

First Blood

If you hang around people in the military very long you hear a lot about "lessons-learned." That's because we learn from our formal training which is based upon the hard lessons learned by our predecessors, and then we work hard at learning from our own real-world experiences. One of those first real-world lessons for me came when my commander took my LDNN interpreter and our Kit Carson scouts out on an operation off the west coast of Vietnam, down south in the war zone called IV Corps.

We were operating out of a little US and Vietnamese riverine patrol boat base called Rach Soi, between the mouths of two rivers, the Cai Bai and the Cai Lon. We knew a lot of enemy weapons were being moved around the area in the canals in small boats at night. The patrol boats operated inland, along the rivers, but some of the activity had to be offshore. We got reports that weapons were being brought in from Cambodia, staged at an island Northwest of our base, then moved onto the mainland and into the U Minh forest. In fact a regular convoy of these little boats seemed to be operating without interference. The boats were about 20ft long, manned by crews of two to four men. We worked out their routes and schedules and started planning ways to intercept this enemy traffic.

Now, in any naval engagement you have to think carefully about how you come up on a target vessel, how you intend to take them down–procedures well documented and tested since the days of the pirates. While the riverine forces had developed these boat searches to a fine art, we SEALs weren't so good at it because we hadn't done much of it yet, let alone out on the open ocean, let alone in the night! But my platoon commander couldn't resist the bait; we knew when and where they were and the chances of interception were good. He decided to go out to attempt an intercept–the first in a series of regrettable lessons to be learned.

We had a little submachine gun in our arsenal loosely called a "hush-puppy," a silenced 9mm weapon with low-powered (subsonic) ammunition intended for close combat without the usual noise, flash, and commotion of conventional firearms. "Why are you taking THAT?" I asked him.

"Well, if we have to do something I don't want to make a lot of noise," he said.

"Jeeze, out at sea, who cares? And, you haven't actually been practicing with this thing, have you? Why not take the weapon you're used to?" But he wanted to take the specialized system, and about ten at night he took his boat, my two Kit Carson scouts, the LDNN interpreter, and a brand-new kid in our platoon, a machine-gunner named P. K. Barnes who was a classmate of mine from Class 54. This was the very first combat operation for young Paul Barnes, a third class petty officer new to the country.

The five of them headed out in our little sampan, an inconspicuous vessel we acquired from the VC during an operation just a few weeks earlier. None of the rest of us felt comfortable with this operation, but he was the boss, and it was his call to make.

They found a suspect VC boat with a potential cargo of weapons around midnight, riding low in the water and with the amidships area well covered. They approached the other boat bow-on, restricting both the vision and fields-of-fire of everybody on the boat except for the LDNN interpreter, Mr. Lac, up in the bow. Barnes survived the next few seconds to tell what happened: they saw two men in the boat. The interpreter stood up, without his weapon readied, and told the other boat in Vietnamese to stop. Instead of stopping, the canvas covering the midsection of the other boat suddenly flies off and two more guys come up, all now firing AK47s. The interpreter was killed immediately. The scout behind him was caught and killed in the same burst of fire. The second Kit Carson scout who was then serving as the sampan coxswain was wounded.

My fearless leader stood up with the little hush-puppy and pulled the trigger. The little submachine gun didn't make a sound–because it didn't fire; the ammo malfunctioned. As he tossed the weapon aside and bent down to grab another weapon he took a round through the leg, and he was out of action. That left the other wounded Kit Carson scout and young Barnes.

Barnes was armed with a light machine-gun used exclusively by SEALs in Vietnam, a 5.56mm automatic weapon called the Stoner which had a rate of fire of 1000 rounds per minute. With his field of fire finally clear, Barnes stood up and fired. "All I could think of," he told me later, "was to stand there and keep shooting until they got me." But they didn't get him, he got them. "All I could see was tracers, people getting hit, chunks of meat and body parts flying in the moonlight, continued Barnes. "Before I knew it there were four dead VC in the other boat, right in front of me and it sank fast. I looked around and everybody else was down, either dead or wounded. So I inflated the lifejackets on all the bodies as our boat slowly settled in the water. Even though we were miles offshore, it was very shallow there, and I could stand up and keep the radio over my head. I knew the MSSC (medium seal support craft) was somewhere within 2mi so I called them. They asked me to light off a flare. So here I am, trying to hold one guy above water, the bodies all floating nearby, the team leader wounded, and trying to keep the radio dry–and this guy wants me to light off a *flare*!"

It's amazing what you can accomplish when you're motivated, and Barnes was full of motivation just then. He lit a flare. The MSSC found them and hauled the remains of the operation aboard. The helicopters came out and lifted the wounded aboard, then transported them back to the nearby Sea Wolf helobase, and took John Marsh and the Kit Carson Scout on to the Navy hospital in Binh Thuy. Barnes came back from his first mission with more combat experience than most SEALs accumulate in a career, some lessons learned, and a recommendation for the Silver Star.

We all learned a lot from that, including the team leader. He told me later, "that was the dumbest thing I ever did." To make matters worse, I had attended the LDNN interpreter's wedding a few weeks before; now I had to go tell his new bride he was dead. And while that platoon leader is still a good friend of mine after almost thirty years, he still has a leg that doesn't function very well.

Inventing Unconventional Warfare, Navy-Style

That was the end of my work with the Kit Carson scouts and the LDNN; two were dead and the other was wounded. Even so, we had been very successful with the idea of force multiplication. We had been very successful at working with the indigenous people. And together with the Vietnamese, we got to be very good at making the VC very nervous. But a lot of the SEALs weren't too comfortable working with the Vietnamese, so they started doing quite a lot of what we call "direct action" missions on their own.

That happened pretty early, before 1967, and even earlier down in the Rung Sat Secret Zone, in the southern part of the RVN. We started sending whole platoons of SEALs over and using them for unilateral operations with perhaps a little support from a few Vietnamese scouts or interpreters. The mission profile changed to an American unit operating when, where, and how its commander wanted. Our guys patrolled aggressively and effectively. It was not uncommon for each

SEAL to go out on sixty to 100 or more missions during a six-month tour.

While the SEALs and the Green Berets were invented to do similar missions, and started out that way, the Green Berets and SEALs evolved during the war in Vietnam into somewhat different forces. For one thing, the Army's Special Forces (the proper name for the people called Green Berets) have always been far more numerous than Navy SEALs. The Army, too, has done a much better job of "force multiplication," working with indigenous peoples, speaking foreign languages, and living in foreign cultures. That is a true evolution of the old OSS mission and what Kennedy had in mind.

SEALs, however, have come to avoid the force multiplication role; we did it in Vietnam, we've done it in the Persian Gulf, but unfortunately it just isn't what we tend to do. We would prefer to be hands on operators. We really like the sneaky "direct action" raids and ambushes, and we do them well. Kennedy had that in mind, too, and I think he'd approve although I believe we should get more into the FID role than we currently are.

Then we started to pull the platoon commitments out of Vietnam. That began about 1969, when we started losing US supporting units. Once again, we came to be used more in the advisory roles. Now a SEAL in a platoon might not go out on more than ten or twelve missions during a six-month rotation. By 1972 the platoon drawdown was pretty much complete although some advisors remained.

We had gone from a mostly advisory role to a mostly direct action role and back to advising again, and we were good at both. We filled a gap in the grand tactical plan, doing ops that the Army couldn't do, the Navy couldn't do, and that the Marines might have been good at . . . if they had dedicated little amphibious patrol teams like ours, which they didn't.

We went out hunting the enemy in twos and threes, something the bigger conventional units couldn't afford, and we found them.

After Action Review

Unlike the Army, we managed to keep our platoons together for deployments and returned to their parent commands. That required bending some Navy SOPs, but it was important and successful. It also required keeping deployments to just six-month temporary duty (TDY) assignments; anything longer risked having guys getting reassigned permanently anywhere rather than their home teams. We knew how to work with each other even before we arrived.

CHAPTER 7

Boats and Boaters, Then and Now

SEALs rely on the support of the boats and their crews that get us in and out of our missions. But these guys aren't SEALs themselves, they are small boat crewmen from the fleet. For a guy coming out of the conventional surface Navy, the change can be quite dramatic. While we are trained and accustomed to considerable austerity, the guys in the fleet normally get three hot meals, showers, a movie every night, and the knowledge that the enemy is far, far away.

But the guys who volunteered to drive the SEALs around are part of the "brown-water" Navy (the riverine units known as Mobile Support Teams or MSTs) and had to be a different breed. We developed a very close relationship with them. They shared most of our hardships and endured a lot of danger. Most of them were terrific.

The NVA Gang That Couldn't Shoot Straight

I had only one problem with an MST boat crew in Vietnam, and it was one of those odd, interesting, memorable experiences that turn into war stories. Here's what happened:

We put together a real unusual operation, deep in the U Minh forest. The plan was to use a MSSC for the insertion; the MSSC is a pretty big boat, with twin 454cid engines and a flat bottom, great for cruising down the big sections of the Mekong River but not too good for moving around the little tributary where we wanted to go. So we towed a Boston Whaler behind the MSSC; once we got close to the area, my team would pile into the smaller boat and go the rest of the way in that. The

MSSC was supposed to stand by while we did our stuff, waiting patiently for our return and serve as a radio relay with their bigger radio.

We saddled up around midnight, moved off into the darkness guided only by radar. This MST (Mobile Support Team) had been providing battlefield taxi service for us for over five months; in just a couple more weeks they were due to go home.

We were all a bit gun-shy at this point. The first night of operations in this area, the MSSC carrying my boss, John Marsh, and his squad got hit by a B40 rocket into the side of the MSSC, slightly wounding the coxswain and disabling the boat's steering. The second operation out the LSSC I was riding in got hit by automatic weapons fire. So the night we towed the Boston Whaler was the third big operation, and we weren't real thrilled about going down this river, but we had to go anyway. And it was a tremendous river, 60ft deep and about a quarter-mile or more wide. Way out in the middle we were pretty safe.

As we moved upstream and started to close on our objective area, about a mile and a half from where we wanted to insert, on the radar I could see fish traps spread across the river ahead of us. We eased up to the traps, invisible and inaudible to anyone on the river or ashore. In fact, the MSSC was a real "stealth" boat that way; you can't hear it at all until it passes, and then the only sound is a gentle burbling not too different from the sound of the river itself.

Just as we started to pass through the line of fish traps it seemed that somebody turned on the daylight–an illumination flare went up from the riverbank, turning the night suddenly to day. Now we could see, and boats were everywhere, all loaded with an NVA unit right in the middle of crossing this river!

The world opened up on us. Rocket-propelled grenades (RPGs) flying left and right. Water spouts all around the boat from mortars, machine guns, RPGs. Tracers everywhere, just like in the movies! We opened up on them with everything we had–our 40mm's, machine-guns, rifles, grenade launchers, the works. "Hit it!" I told the coxswain of the boat who didn't need much encouragement to give it full throttle. We roared through the breech in the fish traps and left the NVA to deal with their disrupted crossing. The engagement seemed to take forever but probably lasted only a few seconds, certainly less than a minute.

Safely upstream, we took inventory. Anybody hit? Nope. Any major damage to the boat? Seems to be okay. In fact, we took only one single bullet hole in an upright stanchion from all that shooting! We had to wonder, had we done the same to them? We were all shaken, and the NVA probably were too.

We kept moving up stream. I had scrambled the Seawolf helicopters, then called them off and had them stand by. But what to do now? By this time, we were only a mile or so from our op area, none of us got hit, so why not proceed with the mission? "Okay with me," my leading petty officer said.

"I'm not going in there, sir," the petty officer at the helm of the boat said. "I am NOT taking this boat anywhere near that shore! I do not want to get killed!"

"The NVA aren't down here," I told him, " they're all back down the river half a mile! They're all on foot–they aren't going to bother us!"

"I don't care–I'm scared and I am not going."

The engineman and the gunner chimed in then, too; they didn't want to go any further. But the warrant officer commanding the boat, CWO3 Ron Fox, said, "I'll take you in."

I thought about this for a few minutes, then said, "No, let's go back to base, there's too many 'what-if' factors here now." But the only way back was the way we'd just come. I called the helicopter gunships and got them overhead, then we headed downstream.

"We know where this place is; I can spot it on radar. When we start through this danger area I will send up a flare while we open up on both river banks as we go through the fish traps. You guys open up on anything that shoots from the bank."

We snuck up on the gap in the floats, the coxswain gave the boat full throttle, and we all cut loose on the banks. There was no return fire, of course; the NVA were long gone.

Over the radio I could hear the gunship pilot laughing hysterically. "What's the problem? Why aren't you shooting?" I demanded.

"Because you guys are putting so much stuff out there no room is left for my bullets to get through!" he called back.

We made it back without further incident. The incident, though, really upset me, partly because of the surprise element of the engagement but more because of the behavior of the seasoned boat crew. This combat-refusal really shook me up and I was deeply disappointed. I pulled them all in, including their officer, and told them, "You guys are scheduled out of here in two weeks but as far as I am concerned you are off duty right now! I don't want to have anything more to do with you. I can't trust you, and I can't have that."

Special Boats and Special Squadrons

While that one incident was a disappointment, I have a lot of respect and affection for the guys in the boat units. They have never, so far as I know, left one of us on the beach somewhere, alive or dead. They deliver us and get us out. Just as SEALs have a tradition of never leaving a weapon or body behind, the boat units never leave SEALs behind. Now, there have been some times when they needed a little help fighting their way back in to get us, but they've always executed the extraction, including many under fire.

We had good boats during the Vietnam era: the STAB

(SEAL Tactical Assault Boat), a 24ft high speed outboard that could handle a squad; the MSSC, the best of the bunch in my opinion, a 36ft inboard/outboard vessel that could handle up to the whole platoon; the PBR, a water jet driven 24ft cabined fire support boat, the LSSC, a 32ft SEAL insertion water-jet drive boat that quite often clogged up on you–especially at the times when you most needed the thing to perform. The MSSC and LSSC are both gone now, replaced by the Mini-ATC and PBL (Patrol Boat, Light)–a riverine patrol and assault boat and a newer version of the old Boston Whaler, respectively.

You hear a lot of criticism of the old boats among the new SEALs–complaints that the MSSC was maintenance-intensive, for example, and fueled with gasoline instead of diesel. The first objection to the MSSC is true; they took a lot of work to keep going. But the fears about fire and explosion from hits on a gasoline-powered boat are just unfounded; it didn't happen once to an MSSC, so far as I know, and they took hits constantly! Furthermore, with self-sealing fuel bladders and new armor technologies, these incidents are even less likely to occur in today's combat situations. Attitudes like that are quite common in NSW these days; they're well-intentioned, but based on a lack of actual combat experience. The operators lose excellent tools, like the MSSC, because of what somebody who's never experienced combat thinks will happen.

But that's nothing new. When SEALs first started operating in Vietnam it was with existing landing craft, vessels designed for conventional units and operations. The "riverine" craft were nothing more than plain old landing craft, LCM-6s (Landing Craft, Mechanized) and LCUs (Landing Craft, Utility) adapted to close-in SEAL support ops with the addition of stand-off chain-link fencing to defeat RPG rounds, armor, and .50cal machine-guns.

While those craft provided support for SEALs, we didn't

own them. We went over with just our little inflatables and a couple of LCPLs (Landing Craft, Personnel, Large); we worked with those, learned from them, adapted them, and came up with new designs. By the end of the war we had a whole fleet of dedicated SpecOps boats. We learned how to get in and out of places and what happens when you neglect to pay attention to the tide and get stuck in the mud. We learned how to ease into the shore and put guys over the bow, into the mud unseen, unheard, and unnoticed. We developed all kinds of tactics–false insertions, for example, that made it tough to know where we were coming ashore. Then, as soon as the war ended, all that was discarded and forgotten as if it would never be used again! We dumped the MSSCs, the LSSCs, and the STABs. We inherited the PBRs, developed the ill-fated Seafox, and then constructed the Mk III Patrol Boat (PB)–plus the Mini-Armored Troop Carrier (ATC), which was another jet boat, formerly owned and operated by the Marines; a slow, cumbersome boat capable of only about 18kt unless you spend lots of dollars for a souped up re-engine job.

Boat speed is important to the life-expectancy of a SEAL; when you get bushwhacked from the bank while you're moving along a river, the "kill-zone" is quite short. If you can accelerate quickly there's a good chance you can escape unharmed. But if the boat stalls (as the LSSC often did) or blunders slowly away (as does the Mini-ATC) the enemy can ping away at your hull for what seems like an eternity.

Special Boat Squadron

There are two Special Boat Squadrons (SBR); SBR-1 on the West Coast and SBR-2 on the East Coast. They each have operational Special Boat Units (SBU) assigned to them. The squadrons are now a full-up major command within NSW. It is a "captain-major-command-billet," even though the unit has one less Special Boat Unit and fewer active duty folks than in the past, when it was commanded by a commander. It is, however, heavily funded and is receiving lots of new hulls. Both coasts will be getting the new Patrol Coastal (PC) ships, Mk V Special Operations Craft (SOC) and the 30ft Rigid-Hull Inflatable Boats (RIBs); the Mk III Patrol Boat will be retired, and the Seafoxes are fortunately gone.

Seafox

The Seafox was part of the SEAL small combatant craft inventory from 1978 to 1993. It was developed in about 1977, just at the end of my tour as the RDT&E officer for Naval Special Warfare Group Two (NSWG-2) in Little Creek. We were in sad need of a replacement for the old 36ft LCPL which had very little capability to insert and extract SEALs for missions. It had been used for decades to drop and pick up UDT swimmers in the old traditional method seen so often on TV and in the movies, but it was slow and not very stable in any sea. The NSW hierarchy decided to budget some money and ask the Navy's architects at the Naval Sea Systems Command to develop a boat that would provide speed, command, control, communications, and firepower to insert and extract Special Oper ations Forces.

The test and evaluation of the prototype craft took place in the vicinity of Little Creek, Virginia. My friend, Tom Coulter, and his platoon did much of the operational test and evaluation (OT&E). He and I discussed the boat shortfalls during and after the tests extensively. We both concluded that any boat that sits at rest with its bow lower than the stern is inherently in trouble before it leaves the pier. At the completion of the test, Tom and I were in the post critique with CAPT Ted Lyons and some of the designers, and other community leaders. Tom told them of an incident of its "bow plunging" when crossing a wake and smashing out the flat windshield ahead of the coxswain's stand. Tom told the audience he was not impressed with the overall capability the boat displayed and being not a shy individual, he stood firm and let his opinion be known. After his recommendation that we not accept the craft, Lyons told him to sit down and keep quiet–that the money had already been appropriated for thirty-six of these craft and that the production would go forward. In the years following, we had numerous bow plunging incidents, numerous mechanical failures, water being absorbed into the fiberglass, and most notably, windshields being smashed, resulting in numerous injuries over the years and one death in 1988 while I was the SBR-1 Commodore. Finally, the Navy woke up and severely limited its use. It has now been replaced by the RIB.

The lesson learned here is that when we ask SEALs to test prospective equipment and there are found to be legitimate problems with the hardware, the leadership needs to listen and address the issues or cancel the program. We simply cannot afford to have dangerous or incapable expensive pieces of equipment produced that have been noted to be flawed.

Patrol Coastal Craft

The Patrol Coastal (PC) craft is a new "commissioned" small ship allegedly dedicated to coastal patrol and interdiction (CPI) and SEAL support. I don't think we really gain anything with it given its cost except a logistical nightmare. Its undermanned, sorely under-gunned, relatively slow, and not as capable for inserting more than a squad of SEALs than the smaller MK V SOC, even though inserting and extracting Special Operations Forces (SOF) is the PC's secondary mission. It is a hull that many in NSW think belongs in the conventional surface fleet. Yes, it did a good job during the Haiti crisis, but had we already had the MK V in inventory it could easily have done the same thing. In fact, even in 1968 the Antelope Class Patrol gunboat (PG class) was a faster, better gunned, more capable craft than we have in the PC today. When we need support from a fast frigate or patrol craft, we have plenty to call on already. Otherwise it seems to make more sense for us to stay in the boat business, not join in the ship business despite the support the PC is getting from the senior leadership.

Mk V Special Operations Craft (SOC)

While the PC hasn't impressed many of us, the new Mk V SOC is a different story. It is a fast, soon-to-be-well-armed boat and appears to be easy to maintain. As its primary mission, it will handle up to sixteen SEALs for a strike mission; it will get you in and out without much fuss or commotion. It is air-transportable (within reason) and therefore can be quickly moved to the area of concern. It is "stealthy" in that it doesn't show up too brightly on radar, something considered into the boat design from the beginning. Without getting into the area of classified information, you can't make a boat with a significant "low-observable" radar signature without designing it that way from the keel up. While that wasn't done with the Mk V, features have been added to this design to approximate low observability. The current weapons system is inadequate and will have to be refitted with a better system once one has been chosen, or it too will remain under-gunned. One of the lessons learned in the Persian Gulf crisis during the Iran-Iraq war was that when you have a patrol boat being used on patrol for more than about 24hr, you need to have a significantly larger crew and the ability to support them. That isn't part of the MK V manning plan.

Rigid-Hull Inflatable Boats (RIB)

The RIBs are the latest addition to the small craft inventory that are used regularly by the SEALs and SBU personnel for everything from diving support to insertion and extraction operations. Both the 24ft and 33ft versions are in the SBU inventory. The future calls for these utilitarian craft to be restricted to the 33ft larger RIB only as they will support most of the short-range operations envisioned. These RIBs do have vulnerabilities. They lack adequate guns for any heavy engagement, and they are susceptable to radar, infrared, and thermal detection systems.

The main advantage of a RIB is its enhanced performance with the rigid hull characteristic. This type hull provides better speed and sea-keeping ability yet retains the safety of the inflatable craft bladders.

Combat Rubber Raiding Craft (CRRC)

These versatile small inflatable 14ft boats are the mainstay of the SEAL detachments. They are owned and operated by the SEALs themselves. They can be rolled up and launched from submarines, placed on pallets and parachuted into the water, and launched from over the side of major vessels at sea. They carry a fire team. And due to their low silhouette they are more difficult to detect by radar and the naked eye when coming over the horizon. What they gain in flexibility, they lose in range, firepower, and speed. But every SEAL is familiar with the operation of this respected little craft.

Boats of the Future

One of the big challenges for SEALs in the future is the problem of infiltrating a group of people from their launch site to the target area undetected. Every little backwater Third World nation today has some kind of surface-search radar.

Even the most basic of these systems can pick up your little boat at great ranges and with good accuracy.

Night vision equipment, once exotic and extremely expensive, is common and cheap today–and highly capable, too. This means we lose some of the protection we've traditionally expected from the "cover of darkness."

Then there are the thermal imaging systems that can see the heat from a boat engine, through dark and fog, at greater ranges than the infiltrator would like.

All of these systems are for sale at bargain prices from commercial manufacturers and from the old Soviet states who have lots of Cold War surplus and a need for ready cash. I have personally heard senior leaders in the community say that there is no need to worry about infiltration through the general threat envelope. Such is simply not the case nowadays. We need to get the leadership and industrial military complex solving these issues for every mobility platform we use. It is one of the critical issues for our viability on the horizon.

CHAPTER 8

Seal Delivery Vehicles (SDV)

So getting in to the target is harder than ever, thanks to advances in and proliferation of detection technology. Our primary response is to apply the same reliance on high technology to defeating these detection systems. And the most exotic of these technological marvels are our sub-surface systems, particularly the SDV.

SDV Operation

It was off the San Clemente Island coastline, and we were tasked to perform a clandestine demolition raid against the pier at the Navy facility for an Operational Readiness Evaluation (ORE). Then PO1 Tom "Mac" McCutchen, a superb SDV pilot, and I went on the operation using the old Emerson Oxygen rebreathers, commonly known but highly overrated as the "death rig." This was in the days when the MK VII Mod 6, forerunner to the current MK VIII, was still using the clear plexiglass canopies. We could, in this earlier version, see out of these canopies if light were available. In fact it was not uncommon to be a passenger and view such sealife as a shark swim by as we motored to an objective. On this particular operation, it was late at night, and the moon was full that evening. The seas were calm, and we launched about 8mi away, over the horizon, using the SDV sled.

The sled is nothing more than a skid that had a cradle that the SDV rested in. When the sled is towed behind a support boat, it comes up on step and permits the SDV to be towed rather quickly from one location to another. Lessons learned the hard way demand the SDV and sled must be watched constantly. Unfortunately, there have been a couple serious incidents where something went wrong and an SDV slid out of the sled while under tow and disappeared somewhere along the track. The losses total over a million dollars.

After launching the SDV, we began motoring in to the northern point of the island from where we would then follow the contour of the island coastline to the pier from about 15-20ft depth. The need to stay shallow was demanded by the use of the Emerson oxygen rebreathers which could cause the divers to encounter a bout of oxygen toxicity if used much deeper. This required having a good pilot who could maintain critical depth control. Mac was such a pilot. As we neared the coast, we began the transit through the kelp beds off the coast. It was phenomenal to have no sounds except the quiet whirring of the electric motor and the flapper valves in your mouthpiece. Outside we could see the kelp forest and the schools of fish swimming as we passed through it with the moonlight backlighting.

Once at the pier, we bottomed out. We could see the guards on the pier, patrolling and watching for us. We swam to the objective, placed the simulated explosives, and then returned to the SDV and transited back. This was the most memorable and beautiful of all the SDV runs I ever made.

Its not always so nice. A few months later, my CO, Dan Hendrickson, tasked us to try to attack a fleet of amphibious ships coming into Camp Pendleton to land a flock of Marines. The idea was to transit to the area offshore from the landing. Lay on the surface until the ships came in and then come near to one and light a flare simulating that we had launched explosives against the major vessels bearing down on us. The thought of what could happen if we got under one of these 300 ft ships coming at 10kt to the shore was in our minds. We set off about 2hr before the scheduled landing and moved to the approximate beach landing site using dead reckoning, which was the only navigation aides we employed other than an occasional surfacing to see landmarks. Again, Tom McCutchen was the pilot. I had just received my new SDV wetsuit which was 3/8in thick in the trunk area and 1/4in thick in the extremities with no zippers. Little did I realize it was a blessing in disguise to have that suit. After 2hr, we surfaced in the approximate area. No ships could be seen because the fog had rolled in, and we were not able to see more than about 50ft away. Now we faced the possibility of not seeing the vessels come in until they were on top of us, literally. We could hear pretty well as there was almost no swell or wave action.

After two more hours, we began to question if we were in the right area as the landing should have taken place 2hr earlier. We then began wondering how to re-link with our mother support vessel. After another hour, miraculously, the little LCPL towing the sled showed up about 50ft away in the fog. They were as surprised as us to see one another in the fog. The landing had been canceled due to the fog, and they had been trying to locate and recover us. For anyone who has swum off the coastline of Southern California even during the summer, temperature does not have to be described. The only difference between summer and winter temperatures is it goes from cold to colder. The total time in the water for Mac and I that operation was just under 6hr. Cold was hardly the word to describe the condition we were in, but the wetsuits proved themselves worthy. We could still function well enough to place the SDV back into the sled.

Advanced SEAL Delivery System (ASDS)

The staff at SPECWARCOM recently, about 1993, made an important decision in concert with the US Special Operations Command (USSOCOM) about this issue, a decision with heavy political connotations; the underwater systems developers have been directed to develop a new SEAL support platform known as the ASDS. This will necessarily keep the submariners busy, and that makes them feel needed, wanted, well-funded, and secure. The submarine community has a lot of political clout in the Navy, a lot of extremely high-value submarines that are currently without much of a mission, and a need to justify its role in the Navy of the future. The more the SEAL community can adapt these vessels and keep them busy the more secure the submariners will be–and the more politically secure NSW will be, too, if the submariners go to bat for us. That is Navy politics, and that's the way these things work.

Now, it will take five or six years to adapt this ASDS mini-sub to our nuclear vessels that will "mother" them and who knows what new high-tech underwater detection systems will be available then? We are putting almost all of our money on a bet on the stealthyness of the ASDS and leaving a large gap in our operational capability between now and then. Furthermore, there will be few of these ASDS available to go around the world. The situation can and should be addressed today by other options.

While we've been putting time, money, and imagination into a system that might come on line around the year 2000 or later, we have neglected addressing surface systems we need today. We could have had systems on the surface that could penetrate nearly any defenses of any place we want to go. We could be using those boats currently; the guys running the ops would be granted a better chance at mission success today. Instead, the decision was made to shift the priority from surface insertion methods to put the emphasis on underwater delivery technologies. I pray for the operators that this decision does not become an albatross between now and IOC (initial operational capability) of the ASDS.

Let me tell you a little about this ASDS and how it is used. This is a little dry submarine, a newer, much more expensive version of the "wet" SDV we use today. While it is an interesting system with useful potential, it has tremendous limitations and restricts SEAL ops fantastically. I like the SDV/ASDS concept and the idea of having a bunch of these things available, but we have suddenly made a major commitment to rely solely on this ASDS platform as the foundation for our ops in the future given the current and projected threat. I don't think it will happen, and here's why:

First, the ASDS has to be brought in close enough to your target to be in range–a tactic that is not a pleasant thought to the submarine skippers who will be supporting us. Second, it needs a specially equipped submarine designed for its support. Only a few subs will be converted, a couple for each coast, so there will be scant few of them to go around. The chances of having the right submarine and an ASDS at the right place for a quick-response mission, six years from now, are slim at best. The ASDS will only hold a maximum of eight SEALs, and the SEALs all must be extremely proficient at diving. This is because they have to be able to exit the ASDS from underwater, infiltrate to the target or shoreside on SCUBA (probably closed-circuit type), carrying all their operational equipment necessary to perform their mission. Then they will likely return the same way to rendezvous with the ASDS to get away, only to potentially draw unwanted attention to the presence of a supporting submarine (read: high value target) in the area.

Furthermore, once the ASDS is launched, there are still all sorts of problems for the SEALs who ride it in on a mission: waterproofing problems for the gear, pressure-proofing problems, the problems of cold and exposure after exiting the

ASDS and after coming ashore. Once ashore, the people on the op and all their gear will be wet and cold because, although they're dry in the ASDV, they have to swim out. Worse, we will not have this available until nearly the year 2000. If we go to war and must rely on this ASDS when it comes on line to penetrate a well protected coastline, only three SEAL ops can be conducted at one time instead of the numerous missions we could execute with specially configured surface craft.

This future system was selected in place of excellent alternatives which could be in use and available for ops right now. This surface system would have made life safer for a lot of guys. It was discarded for what I believe were primarily political rather than practical reasons within our community. There are those that do not share this perception, but I would rather have more choices of ingress and egress than being limited to one anytime.

CHAPTER 9

NSW Politics and the NAVSPECWARCOM Yacht Club

It might come as a surprise to most Americans but we have an odd problem in the SEALs. Very few in our community today have had any significant combat experience at all. We have senior captains who've never personally participated in combat missions in any capacity–never fired a shot or been fired upon. As a result these people make unrealistic decisions and set forth doctrine that is doomed to fail. For example, when we were debating the wisdom of shifting our priorities from surface insertion to subsurface insertion, a senior captain asked me, "Well, what's wrong with just letting the teams lock out of a sub and going in with a CRRC? They are impossible to see at night."

The problem is that you can pick up a CRRC at 2-3mi with a little night-vision device you can buy for about $600. And if the folks who are making the decisions about these things can't equate that cheap little device to the compromise of an insertion, then somebody's "lost the bubble."

Eighty percent of all our ops today depend on surface craft. We have been told that, suddenly, for the tough threats we will start relying on subsurface delivery using systems that aren't available at all now, that will total only three world-wide in the future, and that will have considerable technical and tactical limitations. You have to wonder if somebody's smoking something funny.

I don't think this reliance on ASDS will ever develop as planned. I will bet that we'll still conduct the vast majority of our insertions and extractions on the surface. But if we don't develop ways to deal with the practical, real world threats to these surface ops we won't be able to conduct our missions effectively at all because we won't get past the threat envelope.

Boats are an essential part of SEAL heritage. They can deliver us almost anywhere we are supposed to go. With them we can insert many teams at many locations, simultaneously. The current boats need to be redesigned with modern technologies in mind, adapted for a new world of threats. Instead, we've put most of our insertion technology money on a long-shot bet in a high-stakes game. That is proverbially "putting all our eggs in a single basket" that we don't even hold yet.

1961–1970 The Beginning of the End of Underwater Demolition Teams

At this time in history–from about 1962 until 1970– we had SEAL Team One based in Coronado, SEAL Team Two in Little Creek, plus UDT 21 and 22 in Little Creek; UDT 11, 12, and 13 in Coronado. The SEAL teams, though, were getting involved in what we now call *special operations* or *unconventional warfare operations*–counter-guerrilla warfare, paramilitary operations, and counter-insurgency. We didn't notice it at the time, but a split developed between the UDT and the SEAL commands: conventional operations for UDT and unconventional operations for SEAL teams. Then, in about 1971, UDT 13 and 22 were decommissioned–signaling the beginning of the end of the UDT era.

That began what became a mistake in my opinion. The primary mission of the Underwater Demolition Teams (UDTs) was to provide hydrographic reconnaissance and beach clearance for the amphibious forces of the United States. Until we got rid of UDT 13, half of each West Coast UDT was normally kept forward-deployed at all times–the CO and half the team for one six-month period, followed by the XO and the other half of the team for the next six months. That way we always had people forward-deployed to support the amphibious task force commander for any emergency in the Western Pacific or the Mediterranean. The guys from the East Coast were formed up into platoons and deployed aboard frigates as Amphibious Ready Group (ARG) units. These were conventional forces supporting conventional operations.

But then that changed. Starting about 1972 we set up a NSW unit in Okinawa, at White Beach; then about 1974, it rotated to Subic Bay, in the Philippines. This was in support of Seventh Fleet operations. On the SEAL teams, we were performing both conventional and unconventional missions during this time. We trained our counterparts in other navies–the Koreans, for example.

The Big Drawdown

The big drawdown started about this time, around 1972. Until then we had about 300 people in the SEAL teams, and we had to have that many folks because of all the deployments we were making. Then, one day, twenty four guys were called into personnel and told, with no rhyme or reason we could discern, "You guys are going some place else; you can get out of the Navy, or to a diving billet, an EOD (explosive ordnance disposal) billet, but you are out of here!" Several of my classmates were involved and at least two of them got out of the Navy and went into commercial diving. They, and the rest of the twenty four, were literally tossed out of the SEAL teams–a tremendous morale-buster.

We started to get COs without SEAL experience and platoon leaders who didn't have adequate SEAL training, and who did not lead very well. We had officers going for second or third tours leaving from a UDT who wanted to get their "ticket punched." They would deploy to Vietnam and operate very little–maybe only a dozen operations in a six-month deployment. They weren't interested in operating. I spoke with platoon commanders who said they didn't even think their job included shooting when on an operation–that means with a five man squad, if the other four guys shoot and the officer-in-charge provides direction only, they lose 20 percent of their firepower! A lot of the guys who'd been "plank-owners" or very early members of the SEALs decided that the elite leadership era in the SEAL teams was gone, so they decided to bail out and went to UDT. I was one of them. I left SEAL Team One on 1972 and became the first US SEAL advisor assigned to Korea to the work with the Korean UDT under the Joint United States Military Advisory Group (JUSMAG). That position lasted about a year, and then the Admiral Henry Morgan, a real competent gentleman and the senior Navy officer in Korea, got me involved in coordinating our Navy folks and their Navy folks when we worked together–US Navy SEAL platoons deploying for joint training three or four times each year, joint mine warfare exercises, joint salvage dive training, joint anti-submarine warfare training, and other naval training exercises.

Different Strokes for Different Folks

The SEAL teams' missions, character, and organization started changing pretty radically. While we originally had lieutenants commanding a team, now it was a lieutenant commander–and creeping upward. As the grade of the leadership creeped upward, the size of the units stayed the same or actually shrank!

This, and other alterations, were partially the result of a fundamental change that occurred just a few years earlier, in 1969, when NSW became designated a community, just like the aviators, submariners, and surface warfare professionals. With that change, we all started 2-3yr, closed-loop tours within the community, with a cookie-cutter type career progression laid out to higher rank. So this new community designation, along with the down-sizing at the end of the war in Vietnam and the natural grade creep for individuals who stay aboard, resulted in a kind of top-heavy organization inappropriate to its basic missions.

Command of a SEAL team is a rather over-glorified achievement. While it sounds sexy, actually you only train people and provide a kind of talent pool or "temp agency" for theater commanders. When theaters need SEALs for operations, they call up the teams with a request for people and resources; then the theater commanders get to command and control those SEALs on the missions. Being the commander of the SEAL team is a kind of like being a glorified training officer only having less latitude than when I was a platoon commander.

We are now at the point where we have very senior commanders running SEAL teams–the size of the teams hasn't changed; it's still about 205 people–but now we have XOs who are ready for promotion to commander, or in some cases who already hold commander rank. Compare that to the Army: there, an officer at the 0-5 level (the rank of lieutenant colonel in the Army or commander in the Navy) will typically command a battalion of around 450 people. It's embarrassing, in a way, but the phenomenon is happening throughout the Navy.

While it is certainly true that a SEAL team commander has lots of responsibility, it is also true that we now have superb long-range communications that allows the commander to talk to his bosses from anywhere in the world, with superb clarity and complete security.

And the guys out in the field, commanding the missions and acting autonomously, are still lieutenants–just as they've always been! The guy who's the training commander, who "chops" them to the operational forces and sends them to the field, is the CO and senior administrator, and he just doesn't need to be such a senior officer.

Now, SEAL-team COs are normally in an administrative role unless we're in the field, unless we get "chopped" to somebody's theater command. When we go to the Middle East for something like Desert Storm, we go as tactical task unit commanders reporting to the theater commander.

Very few of the more senior folks ever operate–or want to operate–once they hit senior rank. In other communities, senior pilots, including CO's and XO's still lead the wing on a mission, senior ship drivers still drive ships and submariners still submerge subs. Senior officers in the SEALs tend to hide behind desks. I find this offensive. I felt that as I became more senior, I was better mentally, more capable, and certainly could shoot as straight. At a time when we are best able to lead from the front, why do we quit operating?

Pirates 17, US Navy 0

Then, in 1975, came the *Mayaguez* incident. We weren't involved in the actual attempt at rescue of the hostages–the Marines got tapped for that–the SEALs got tapped to bring out the bodies of the dead Marines.

Now, in case you've forgotten, the *Mayaguez* was an American freighter captured by Malaysian pirates; the crew were taken off the ship to a remote island and held for ransom. President Gerald Ford turned the US military loose on the pirates. The operation was a classic ad-hoc fiasco: the Marines assaulted the beach without adequate intel and without any pre-assault fire support. The pirates had a few machine-guns emplaced on the beach, and these weapons mowed down the Marines; the assault was repulsed, plus seventeen Marine dead remained on the shore.

A friend of mine, then LTJG Tom Coulter, commanded

the SEAL platoon that got tasked by the Seventh Fleet admiral to go back for the bodies. As an example of the confused leadership of that time, Tom got a call from the admiral and was told to take an SDV, drive into the beach, and crawl up on the beach and bring the bodies back. Tom said, "Nope, I'm not going to do that!"

"Why not?" the admiral wanted to know.

"Because, sir, if there are already seventeen dead Marines up on that beach, they are dead because somebody did something wrong. Am I supposed to go up there and exchange one dead SEAL for one dead Marine? I am not going to add to the body count. We'd better come up with some other plan—because we aren't going to do it that way!"

Naturally some yelling and screaming ensued at this point down the chain of command. But when it was over the admiral's staff conceded that Tom was essentially correct about the prospects for success. Ultimately, the ship, crew, and hostages were retrieved by negotiations—but the incident was one of the first in a long and unpleasant lessons-learned about dealing with terrorists.

One of the lessons of this incident was an old one, often learned and often forgotten: under the best of circumstances you should have a 5:1 advantage to assault a hostile beach. The Marines assaulted with perhaps a platoon—about forty-five guys—against an enemy entrenched in prepared bunkers and fighting positions. How did this happen? By forgetting all the lessons we'd just learned in Vietnam and earlier wars and by underestimating our enemy. This was just another in a long series of embarrassments, another failed mission.

Change of Mission

It didn't happen right away, but NSW was transformed by events like the *Mayaguez* incident and the failed attempt to rescue the American hostages held by Iran. These failures set the stage–and produced the commitment to get serious about the counter-terror (CT) mission. Nobody would have guessed it at the time, but these were blessings in disguise.

The failure of the rescue mission in Iran in 1980 was the last straw for the Congress; the government said, in effect, "If we are going to have you do this kind of thing, let's set up a response force or forces properly; we don't want any more of these fiascoes."

There were, of course, a whole collection of errors on the attempt to rescue the American hostages in Tehran, Iran: the helicopters came from a Navy mine-countermeasures unit–but were given to Marine helicopter pilots to fly. The Air Force C-130s were there to pick up the folks in the desert. NSW was almost completely excluded, except for the deployment of a few SEALs sent into Iran to provide standby support preparation for the operation. Some of these guys (and a few are associates of mine) actually went into downtown Tehran to help set up the intel and exfiltration.

About this time SEALs started doing some really smart, interesting training in the NATO and Atlantic theaters: we started moving around in civilian clothes, training for covert operations behind the lines. We set up and worked with support networks, E&E (escape and evasion) networks, and we started getting smart about going into foreign areas. All that involved looking like people who weren't in the US Navy and doing things that people in the US Navy weren't supposed to do. In fact, at SEAL Team Two we were running simulated downed Navy pilot E&E nets through "safe houses" out of islands in the Caribbean. We started getting back in the intel business, learning what good intelligence can do for you. It was really good training.

MOB Six

A guy by the name of Dick Marcinko (who you will hear more about later) was the Navy's "point man" for the development of a counter-terror capability for Naval Special Warfare, a process that began about 1979. Even before the SEALs' official CT unit or the later Red Cell unit was formalized, a small group of SEALs was selected for a new unit that would develop techniques for dealing with terrorists on the high seas and anywhere else they might show their ugly little heads. It was called, then, Mob Six. That small unit ultimately developed into a tactical unit and a separate command.

It was a very small, select group. Norm Carley, now a partner of mine, was one of the early leaders in this unit. The learning curve for all of them was extremely steep. Norm helped develop tactics and techniques for boarding ships underway, for taking down oil rigs, ships and aircraft, and for assaulting positions along a waterfront that would normally be inaccessible. They learned how to break into secure compounds in new and novel ways. Most of these techniques I can't describe because they're still in use, but one resultant development I can mention is the insertion technique called "fast-roping;" Before this technique was developed, we rappelled from helicopters. Rappelling is painfully slow and dangerous. But fast-roping allows an operator to drop 90ft in about four seconds. You burn your gloves off, but you get on the ground in a hurry, ready to fight. That's just one of the things that came out of Mob Six's early work, and it is used not just by SEALs but by the Army and Marine Corps, too.

UDT and the Hydrographic Recon Mission–

Then, in 1983, the decision was made to get rid of UDT. It happened in a kind of odd way, and since I had been a detailer near the time, I got to work with the planning board to make the conversion for all the people in UDT to other careers and communities. The most unfortunate excuse offered for getting rid of the units was that some UDT personnel had complained of "second-class" citizen status–that the SEALs were getting the glory, in other words. Well, remember that this was a warm and fuzzy period for the military, and the senior leadership at the time said something like, "We need to make everybody equal, so nobody feels like a second-class member of the community." I suspect that some of these decision-makers had missed being a SEAL themselves.

Well, this was horrible. As soon as the change was mandated, guys who had always been superlative members of the UDT side of the organization–great divers, terrific cartographers, with superb hydrographic reconnaissance skills–were told "you will now be a SEAL." The problem was that a lot of them just didn't want to be SEALs; they had been perfectly happy doing UDT work and being members of the Underwater Demolition Teams. Now, we'd go off on deployments with people who really weren't all that excited about the SEAL mission; they didn't want to be there but were reluctant to say so. It was apparent that a lot were thinking, *well, I don't think I really want to be here but I had better not say anything about it–but if this unit goes to war, forget it–I will be out of here in a heartbeat!*

At the same time the SEAL community absorbed the UDT people, SEALs took on the UDT mission. Suddenly we have guys in the teams who used to be full-time hydrographic recon specialists–and now they're part-timers in carrying out the same mission. And since the UDT-stigma was now confirmed by events, that the UDT specialists really were second-class citizens after all, those SEALs who were tasked to the ARG, with its hydrographic recon mission and traditional UDT assignments, started to think of themselves as second-class members of the NSW community. Now a lot of the best men started scrambling to stay away from the ARG platoons. What a mess!

Amphibious Ready Group (ARG) Platoons

Now, in case you don't know about the ARG platoons, this is an assignment for SEALs that "chops" a SEAL platoon to support a US Marine Corps and amphibious task force. These Marine and Navy units routinely conduct six-month "floats" in the western Pacific and elsewhere across the globe; part of the float involves routine training, but at the same time this force is forward-deployed, ready for combat, complete with all the heavy hardware to conduct a brigade-sized assault across a beach. These amphibious assaults need good hydrographic and beach surveys–the old UDT job–and that's now tasked to the SEALS, along with the Very Shallow Water Mine Countermeasures tasking, whether we like the idea or not. So we send a platoon of SEALs along with each of these deployments, plus a fairly senior SEAL liaison officer. This ARG platoon is expected to perform pre-invasion surveys, plus across-the-beach operations (taking down a radar site, for example, or using a laser-designator to guide precision munitions toward high-value targets). While the Marines' excellent Force Recon units can do across-the-beach ops and use laser-designators, they aren't prepared to do hydrographic recon; that's still strictly our assignment.

The ARG platoons have an odd reputation for being far from the action but if you look at the record, these forward-deployed SEALs seem to be first on-scene for all the recent 911 calls: the evacuation of Beirut, the pre-invasion survey on Grenada, and they were first in after the invasion of Kuwait in 1989. It was the ARG platoon that took down the *Iran Ajr* after it was caught laying mines in the Persian Gulf.

The result of the low status of the ARG assignment is a

mission-degradation process that continues– despite what SPECWARCOM will tell you–today. We are not nearly as good at the beach survey and hydrographic recon mission today as we were ten or fifteen years ago. The finely honed capability was eliminated with the UDT organization dedicated to completing those specialized missions. We are, however, attempting to counterbalance the loss of expertise by developing better technologies to address these missions.

Another unfortunate thing happened as a result: since we are SEALs, we now specialize in unconventional warfare operations, not conventional forces and conventional operations. While we are still in the Navy–our paycheck still reads the Department of the Navy–our focus now is much more on the kind of *joint* tasking and joint operations rather than just Navy operations. That kind of semi-isolation from the Navy community isn't really healthy for us but it has been a fact of life for a long time.

Grenada

By 1983 the NSW community had pretty well forgotten all about the hydrographic recon mission and was focused intently on the CT mission. We haven't given much thought to beach landings or over-the-beach operations; those were thought to be the old, obsolete, tactics of another era and ancient wars. We were thinking, in the early 1980s, that when we go to war it will be by parachute or helicopter, deep inland, on top of some hapless little compound owned by a few terrorists. Quite suddenly, our community was told to help capture the island of Grenada. This was a shock to people who'd been concentrating on an entirely different mission.

But we had an ARG platoon down there, with then LT Mike Walsh in command. They went in on one side of the island and did a good survey and recon, but that success was completely overshadowed by the fiasco on the other side, when we tried to execute a very flawed mission.

Suddenly, we are supposed to put people on a hostile shore to support a conventional amphibious assault. Hmm, we thought, now how did we used to do that?

Well, we used to do it in a pretty simple, straightforward manner, coming ashore in small boats launched from ships a few miles off the coast. But with all the training for the CT mission, that seemed too simple and primitive. The decision was made to drop the team and its boats into the water by parachute.

The op was a classic goat-screw. The drop was planned for last-light but by the time the boats and SEALs departed the aircraft it was already fully dark. Although two aircraft were supporting the operation, no effective coordination between them was set up; they could have been 500 meters apart or 2,000 when they dropped the team into inky blackness. None of the boats or the SEALs had any form of illumination to help with link-up. The sea conditions were worse than forecast. The SEALs were all overloaded, or under-buoyed, with personal weapons and equipment. They had trained with the fancy, High Altitude-Low Opening (HALO) "Jeddi Knight" parachutes, but then had to jump with the old standard MC1-1 rig, which is set up quite differently, so they weren't re-accustomed to the release procedure. It was, as we say, not pretty: chutes tangled, people got dragged under water, and none of the SEALs on the mission knew where anybody else was. The destroyer standing by to support the SEALs couldn't see a thing. One of the survivors told me, "It was the most horrifying experience of my life–I figured I was dead. We were getting dragged through the water at such high speed that I had a terrible time operating the release. The parachutes were ones we didn't usually use. I know one of the other guys was still alive–I could hear him calling, and he fired his weapon three times. Even while we were getting picked up, I could still hear him . . . but we never found him." We lost four guys, dead, in that drop, and we never recovered the bodies.

One of the two boats was recovered. The engine wouldn't start. The guys couldn't figure out how to now get ashore to begin doing the mission they'd been assigned! Well, miraculously, two alternate boats are suddenly produced by the support vessel–which makes me and some other guys ask, why did they have to jump in to begin with? Stubblefield's Cardinal Rule #1: *Don't Parachute Unless You Have To.* Cardinal Rule #2: *Even If You Find You Have To Jump, Find Another Way.*

Then, another element of SEALs had another mission that involved a helicopter insertion; pre-dawn, inland. Somebody looked at a map and intel photos of the landing zone (LZ) and said, "You can't go in there–that's a hillside, and it is too steep for the helicopters." But the intel officers ignored the observation and stayed with the original plan. And, since delay in these things seemed to be a constant factor, the helicopter insertion that was supposed to come off in the pre-dawn actually went in after daylight. As the helicopters tried to get the teams in, ZSU-23-4 antiaircraft guns started putting holes in the airframes.

One of the operational elements assigned to secure the radio station was quite lucky once they got on the ground. Even though they got shot up and pushed out of the radio station they were supposed to attack, they managed to make it back to the beach and swim out to sea without losing anybody. One, Kim Erskine, still has a chunk of his arm missing from this adventure.

Then there was the group of our guys who were supposed to rescue the governor; they got pinned down for 24hr, were almost out of ammunition, and had to get rescued themselves by the Marines. It could have been worse–the primary radio for the operation got left on the first helicopter by the team leader, Billy Davis, when the excitement of the hot insertion caused him to brainlock (the second helo got shot up on the way in and never made it), and the only communication system available to the operation was one of the little MX-300 short-range squad radios. An enterprising young petty officer was present with a phone credit card that permitted them to place a long distance call from the governor's mansion to the op center at Fort Bragg to relay the status. After that, a radio relay was established to assist the communications out of the mansion.

But not all the SEAL missions got screwed up during the assault on Grenada; as I mentioned earlier, one group performed their mission just as advertised–the ARG platoon, those lowly, second-class, low status SEALs. They showed up, did their job the way it was supposed to be done, then stood down. It occurred to me that in nearly every one of these kinds of situations the US Navy has participated in over the last ten years or so, it has been the ARG platoons that get called first and that go in to execute the first critical part of the mission. That's odd since so many SEALs tend to traditionally shun these ARG assignments, avoiding the months of ship-board forward deployment . . . because some of us are afraid we'll miss the "real action" when something happens. The way it has turned out, these are the guys who've been closest to the action and the ones who seem to have been best prepared to execute when called on.

The guys who jumped in on Grenada were trying to link up with a US warship. That warship had been in Barbados just a few hours earlier–why didn't we just fly them to Barbados and let them walk aboard the ship, then insert from over the horizon? There was no need for a drop, particularly in those winds, especially at night, and certainly not without some lights rigged on the boats and the people!

After it was all over we studied the operation, and it was mostly a real embarrassment. The guys who should have done the over-the-beach recon and perhaps even the radio station were SEAL Team Two–they do over-the-beach operations all the time, and they didn't get called to do anything! Instead, the guys from the CT unit, who'd been working on the counter-terror mission, were sent in, maybe because of all the money that had been invested in their training and equipment. That was a major error. We took guys who'd been concentrating on taking down compounds, terrorists, and airplanes and then told them to do a traditional over-the-beach operation . . . of course they weren't going to be as familiar or good at it despite being very good operators.

That mistake was compounded by another odd conclusion: instead of deciding to use SEAL Team Two type guys for future over-the-beach missions, the sort of thing they train for, our community subsequently decided that we had to make sure the CT guys were trained in beach ops. What's the matter with having the CT specialists stick to their mission, and the over-the-beach specialists used for that kind of operation? Certainly the CT mission is so difficult as to demand that full attention be paid to it. Well, if you ask some of the senior commanders, they will tell you it's because these CT guys are like thoroughbred race horses; they have been trained to this incredibly high level of proficiency and need to be used real-world once in a while to keep up their motivation.

We learned a lot from Grenada. One of my good friends and a very competent warrior, Bob Gormly, commanded the CT unit at this time, and he tried to go in with his team on the mission to rescue the governor. He was on the second bird, though, and it got shot off the LZ. Bob and I may disagree about this, but I think that if you've only got two or three platoons on the ground, the commander needs to be where he can provide best command and control to all the elements, not on the ground. It would be different if the entire unit were on that one operation–but it wasn't–and the commander's leadership is important for the other ops going off about the same time. As it turned out, Bob didn't get to help with the governor's house rescue OR the other missions because he was in a shot-up helicopter unable to join the party on the ground. Of course, it was most likely a political decision for Bob to be on that mission–after all, the whole takeover of the island was to have been a "walk in the park."

Another lesson learned on Grenada was that our inter-service communications were horrendous! The Marines couldn't talk to the Army, and the Army couldn't talk to the Navy–that was a real shock. Still a further lesson learned was that this whole operation had been "war-gamed" as a command-post-exercise (CPX) just a few months earlier; that CPX was sitting on a shelf, complete with all the same lessons-learned, and was totally ignored.

Then, there was the old *I Want My Medal* syndrome; everybody wanted to get a piece of the action and the anticipated glory. The planners, as a result, carved up the operation to let everybody play equally, instead of doing the appropriate thing–turning the whole op over to the Marine Corps, who really are supposed to be the professionals at this kind of thing. The Army didn't need to be there, and the Navy didn't either, except to support the Marines. Alternatively, the Army's 82nd Airborne Division could have jumped in, airlanded the follow-on forces, and done the whole thing themselves, too, without the Marines. One of the things we know about good command-and-control is that you need to preserve unit integrity. This was the same lessons we were supposed to have learned out at Desert One on the failed attempt to rescue the hostages in Tehran, where everybody wanted a slice of the action, where

Marines flew Navy helicopters and tried to coordinate with Air Force transports with Army people aboard. It didn't work properly then, either.

A lot of SEALs were very upset that we lost four guys killed *administratively,* even before we closed with the enemy. We train to NEVER drop into a drop zone (DZ) that's a black hole, with high winds over 20kt, with no lights on people or boats, with people overloaded with gear–we just don't do it. But somebody in the leadership got pressured and forgot to say "no." Leadership is a lot more than just telling people *how* to do something, it sometimes includes telling senior people they *can't* do something. We never did get the bodies back.

We learned a lot from this experience, and we talked about it a lot. The formal after-action-review (AAR) generally gave everybody glowing reviews. The AAR called for more work on communications and interoperability. But the Navy didn't really bother with a full-up analysis until 1993 when it contracted with our prime contractor and my company to do a full case study of the NSW involvement in Urgent Fury. We pulled all the classified records and extensive interviews and studied them all. And even my partner, Norm Carley who helped with the review, was shocked at what we learned during the study. The report, of course, is classified, but it isn't pretty. To sum it up, though, there were a whole series of errors, the worst of which was an unnecessary night parachute jump under what should have become "no-go" conditions. Let's learn by our mistakes and avoid them in the future!

Spies, Spooks and Saboteurs– NSW Kinky and Covert Ops

The NSW community has endured pretty extreme evolutions over the past half century. We started, you'll remember, as combat swimmers, the "frogmen" of World War II who surveyed beaches and cleared obstacles in support of amphibious ops. Then, in Korea, we started doing a few raids and strike missions on the far side of the beach. Then in Vietnam we started going on small unit strike missions, particularly ambushes. After Vietnam we really downplayed the UDT combat swimmer missions, particularly the original beach survey assignment, and started getting into the exotic world of SpecOps–joining the Army's Green Berets and legendary Delta in CT missions.

But besides these basic, well-documented taskings, the SEALs are a "talent pool" for much more exotic and highly classified operations. You hear whispers about these missions in the popular press, and sometimes you read books about them by recently retired (or jailed) members of the community or by reporters with overactive imaginations. Let me give you an unclassified briefing on SEALs' role in clandestine and covert ops.

We do two kinds of `spooky' operations: clandestine and covert. *Clandestine* operations involve SEALs in missions where everybody wears uniforms, carries ID cards, and tries hard to not be observed; but our identity is obvious–if you catch us. Nearly everything a US Navy SEAL does during a career will be of an overt or clandestine nature.

Covert operations involve missions where we don't look anything like US Navy SEALs (we sincerely hope) and where there are no uniforms, no ID cards, and no connection to the armed forces or government of the United States. Few SEALs, maybe one SEAL out of 200, will ever go on a real-world covert mission. It is difficult to give you an example, but there are times when the government wants to take some kind of direct action without publicizing it, and I have done such missions.

Because of our talents in and around the water, there are times and circumstances where we get pulled out of our units to do something to enhance or support national security. When that happens we get attached to some other organization, as a cover, an aircraft carrier, for instance, or some kind of independent duty. Our personnel file goes to the cover organization, but we go someplace else.

Here's an example. One friend of mine spent a lot of time bumming around the Caribbean in a sailboat, acting like a rich boy having a good time. He spent a lot of time in the same little harbors frequented by the drug runners. While he looked like an innocent boat bum on an extended vacation, he was actually providing intel reports from behind the lines of the drug war. While there are tight restrictions (called *posse comitatus*) on the use of SEALs or other members of the US armed forces in direct action non-military operations, there is nothing to prevent our use in the covert collection of information on this kind of problem. In fact, we do a lot of it. But the enforcement is up to civil authorities.

These ops are sometimes extremely dangerous. If you don't play your role perfectly you can get yourself in deep trouble. You'd think this would be worth big bonus points at promotion time, but it doesn't always work that way. During the time you are assigned to these type activities, your personnel file is usually classified. The promotion board generally doesn't get to review the file on your covert operation assignment, so there is a "black hole" during that period where it might look like you were snoozing on the beach, rather than the heroic deeds of daring you were actually performing.

The procedures for this kind of duty have been refined and improved over the years. There are oversight and watchdog groups that monitor these assignments and one thing they do now is try to insure you don't take a career "hit" for doing something good for your country.

Those of us in the NSW community get called on to do two kinds of covert operations: one is as formal members of the

Navy and as SEALs, the other involves assignments for departments outside the DoD. We are sometimes called on to do things in support of the national security interests that involve work for other branches of government.

Part of this work involves intelligence collection. For a long time the government was extremely concerned with what was happening with the traditional adversaries of the United States. Data was collected on those subjects in lots of ways–some of which we helped with. The specifics are still classified, and likely to stay that way–and I have a contract with the Navy to not discuss classified information. But I can give you some general ideas about what we do and how we do it.

After the Grenada op we had some people watching what was happening on the Caribbean nations–Cuba, Haiti, Guatemala, Grenada, and Belize–because all sorts of things were changing, and it was (and always is) important to be aware of any change that might influence a future operation.

In fact, we get involved in all sort of things: when the British executed their mission to retake the Falkland Islands we provided our formal English speaking allies intelligence information, supplies, and "overhead" photography from satellites to help our allies. We didn't (as far as I know) have anybody on the ground with the Brits, but we learn things from these relationships and these quiet little operations. We should have learned, for instance, from the British experience in the Falklands, to avoid using ships that burn easily in a combat theater. The lessons learned by the British should have helped prevent serious damages when an Exocet missile hit on one of our warships in the Persian Gulf. We had to learn it all over, for ourselves, in the Gulf in 1988

Dick Marcinko's Charm School

All this set the stage for a real professional "Golden Age"

for NSW, both on the civilian side of the government and in the SEAL/UDT community. For many of us who considered ourselves special warfare professionals, we finally had an opportunity to put in one pool all the ideas for training, policy, planning, equipment, and mission execution that had been impossible until then. And one of the people with the most imaginative ideas, the greatest enthusiasm, and the highest commitment to the new mission was the aforementioned Dick Marcinko.

Now, you'll never know the names of most people in my profession; we like to call ourselves "quiet professionals," and most of us like being pretty much invisible. Dick was pretty much invisible, too, for most of his career except when he was butting heads with our leadership or somebody on the conventional side of the house. Of course, Dick is a celebrity author now; one of his books, ROGUE WARRIOR has been a best seller for a long time, with good reason. To the layman, it is an adventure "tell-all" story, and it tells a story nobody else could or would tell about our little community. It isn't often that a senior officer in the SEALs gets a courts-martial, but Dick did, and it made the front pages of the newspapers. Then Dick told his own version of the story in his book, and it became a runaway best seller. You'd think that a "tell-all" book about our community would infuriate all of us who constantly preach about the need for secrecy and security, but that's not the way many feel about Dick or his book. A lot of people who read the book, including lots of folks in the Navy, get a very bad impression of both Dick and NSW. But Dick is generally still revered in our community by those who worked for him at one time or another for his commitment, his imagination, and his loyalty to his men. There are a number of guys on the teams who still think Marcinko got screwed by the Navy.

Dick is both revered and reviled by people in the Navy

because he was a leader in the development of our community, a visionary who helped construct today's NSW capability–and he was tried and convicted of major crimes, for which he has done jail time. Within our little community, among those who worked with Dick and who knew him, there are two basic attitudes toward the guy: you either love him or hate him. I, however, am in the middle, and I will tell you about Dick. He and I worked together, shared a house, drank together.

Back around 1977 the United States was the target of a growing number of terrorist incidents. It was pretty obvious that a lot of important people and installations that we'd considered safe before now looked quite vulnerable. The first guy to really recognize this threat was sitting at a desk at OP 0-6 in the Navy's Planning Branch at the Pentagon, CDR. Richard Marcinko.

Dick was a bright guy, respected by his boss, VADM. "Ace" Lyons. Neither Dick Marcinko nor the admiral had graduated from charm school; both were abrasive, impatient, plain-spoken, hard-charging guys. Both were real operators, and I thought a lot of their enthusiasm and drive to make something happen. Dick worked for the admiral, and the two were made for each other; Dick told his boss what he *needed* to hear, not necessarily the answer he wanted to hear. When the concept of a military unit to conduct CT operations was being planned within the DoD, Dick was right in the middle of the planning. He foresaw the need for SEALs to be involved in such missions, and volunteered to set up and lead the Navy's part of the show. He got the job.

Until this time, the CT mission was pretty much the sole responsibility of the Army Special Forces' detachment Delta, developed and led by Col. Charlie Beckwith–another charm-school dropout with a can-do reputation as an operator. Dick was the perfect–and only–guy in the perfect spot at the perfect time to get the Navy involved in this new mission. With the support of the best admiral for the job behind him. Dick put together a "business plan" for the Navy's role in CT operations.

It was a great plan. We thought at the time that he drastically over-estimated the number of people he'd need for support, but as it turned out he might have been a little on the low side. We were used to very few support people but he was estimating something like one-to-one. But the funding prospects were lavish, and he got it approved.

Dick had the vision to see beyond the normal SEAL tactics and operational methods. He realized we'd need to be able to go on a wharf and look like a normal longshoreman rather than like a US Navy SEAL if we realistically expected to fight and win against terrorists. That meant these CT SEALs would have to look like all the other longshoremen, including long hair, civilian clothes–and earrings, if necessary. It was good in theory, although there were some glitches.

Dick's longshoremen tended to be muscle-bound young lunks instead of beer-bellied, beer drinking older union types, the way most dock workers really are. They didn't talk the same, dress quite right, or look quite right. Dick had the right idea but since he hadn't done covert ops previously there was a learning curve to the experience.

The unit was supposed to be extremely secret, but we all knew and observed what was happening anyway. When the guys you work with every day suddenly evaporate from your unit and appear at another place down the street you're going to wonder what's happening. Then, when he shows up at our team bar with long hair and looking a little like a civilian–but his car still has all the military stickers needed to get on the base, along with a green ID card, you start to put two and two together. The ruse starts to fall apart. We never were quite able to be both SEALs and civilians at the same time (and we don't try anymore, either). It might be possible to pull this off in the real world, but not when you've got this secret unit trying to work alongside normal units on a normal base. The big secret was pretty common knowledge.

Red Cell

Red Cell was a sexy cover name for the Navy Security Coordination Team (NSCT), a program that was a great idea and that did a lot of good for the Navy, and at a time when it needed to be done. Security at Navy installations at the time (beginning in 1984) was just dismal! Nuclear weapons storage facilities, submarines, aircraft carriers, and all kinds of high-value targets were just about wide open to terrorist attack at the time. Almost anybody could penetrate the security arrangements to either blow up or capture anything or anybody we had. I had just finished a special assignment (that I can't discuss) and was getting ready to go take command of SEAL Team Three. There was, however, a gap between these assignments of a couple of months with nothing to do; to keep me out of trouble I was detailed to the Red Cell project office in the Pentagon. I developed outlines for the Navy CT manual and wrote other papers to support the project. Dick was in and out of the office then, in-between terrorizing US Navy bases.

The idea behind the program was to set up a small group of guys–about two dozen–to role-play the bad guys and to send them against these installations, to dramatically test existing procedures and to then coach the installation commanders and security staff to develop more effective methods against terrorists. Like all sorts of other Navy training, Red Cell was designed to test, evaluate, and train all the people responsible for the security of US Navy installations worldwide. And, unlike a normal terrorist attack, Red Cell operations were scheduled and virtually advertised to the bases.

Contracted technicians set up video cameras all over the installation, focused on the front gate, the fences, guard houses, the ammunition storage bunkers–all kinds of locations where Marcinko's little band of pirates might strike. Those cameras stayed in full view for at least a few days, until everybody got used to them and got back to a normal routine. Then, in novel places and imaginative ways, Red Cell struck.

They would use forged ID cards to get aboard, or pizza delivery trucks, or diversions. They'd set off an explosion on one side of the base and as soon as all the security forces roared off toward the smoke, they'd climb over the fence on the other, suddenly unguarded side. They would make fools of the Marines and Navy or contract security element for a while, then pull them all in for a "lessons-learned" session, the evaluation and training phases of the exercise.

They'd run the video tape and show everybody the mistakes they'd made. They'd show the success stories, too, although those were few and far between at first. It was embarrassing. Careers were felt to have suffered. Enemies were made, and the guys in Red Cell were not much appreciated. The weak spots in the security plans were identified and recommendations made for tightening things up.

Red Cell was a good, valid idea that began to get out of control. The role-players started to take their roles a little too seriously and began to abuse the program. In some ways, they actually became terrorists. There were occasions when they would drink while on these exercises, the drinking generated some errors in judgment, and real abuses occurred.

One example involved a rather senior base official who was "captured" and became a real hostage. His head was placed in a toilet, among other indignities, as part of Red Cell's testing and evaluation process. This took the concept way beyond any practical application and was the kind of thing that ultimately got Dick in trouble.

Red Cell survived for several years after Dick's fall from grace; in a more reasonable, subdued format it continued until about 1992. Tom Tarbox, a well respected Naval Reservist and personal friend who had already retired as a captain with over twenty years active time, was pulled back to active duty for a couple more years to run this show, but it had been badly wounded by the excesses and gradually faded away.

And that's unfortunate because the concept was and still is sound. We had, and still have, major security problems that ought to be addressed. But a program that demonstrates that lax security exists inevitably embarrasses the commander of the installation and sometimes people higher. You don't make friends and allies that way–even if you don't put their heads in the toilet. Red Cell never left anybody feeling all warm and fuzzy, except perhaps Dick and his desperadoes. So NSCT and Red Cell faded away, and that's too bad. We should still use it to test and validate our security precautions today.

Dick and his Red Cell program, his best-selling books, and now his video tapes provoke a lot of heated discussion among SEALs. You will find many people, especially those who worked with him on Red Cell or his last command who admire him tremendously. When sober, he could often be a charming, brilliant, intuitive, constructive officer. Dick's work to improve the security of our installations at a vulnerable time, his commitment to his mission, and his loyalty to his subordinates, all earned him a lot of support and admiration.

Then there is another group of SEALs who will never forget or forgive him for giving us a black eye after the abuses and excesses of his training operation. He is the best known member of the US Navy SEALs–a self-proclaimed rogue warrior, not the "quiet professional" we like to say we are. He is faulted for being a drunk, a "legend in his own mind." Many people don't believe his war stories and his account of his own exploits. He committed the military sin of ignoring the command and control direction from his senior commanders in NSW. He challenged our community to a duel, and inevitably lost the battle but maybe not the war. If Dick Marcinko had never taken a drink I believe he would be a senior admiral today. He was an operator who wanted to lead from the front. Despite his disgrace, he made tremendous positive contributions to NSW–better tactics, training, and leadership abound because of him.

Operation EARNEST WILL and the Pillars of Hercules

One of the highlights of my career in NSW was during Operation Earnest Will. From 1987 to 1989 the United States provided security for ship traffic coming and going from the Persian Gulf. Iran and Iraq had been slugging it out, shooting up just about anybody in range of their aircraft or naval forces. That included gunboat, mine, and missile attacks on civilian oil tankers from many nations–a condition the US and UN decided was quite unacceptable. The US Navy was tasked with escort for these civilian vessels, a supporting operation called Earnest Will.

The SEALs sent over a Task Group commander and a two task units (NSWG-Middle East, NSWTU-Pacific, and NSWTU-Atlantic). We were based on two big barges, the *Hercules* and the *Wimbrown 7.* We were there for about two and a half years, rotating people in and out on three-to four-month deployments. That was one of the smoothest, well-run joint operations I have seen during my career. Everybody involved did a very credible job.

Norm Carley and I were both over there at the same time; he had one barge, I had the other. Norm's barge, the *Hercules* , had been the foundation for the largest floating crane in the world–275ft long, 175ft beam–just immense! He had helicopter hangers and decks, plus lots of working and living spaces below deck. The barge had a full-service galley, left over from prior service with the oil companies. One huge and one large crane each provided heavy lift for almost anything smaller than an aircraft carrier. This barge was so big that you couldn't notice any movement from the sometimes large swells in the northern Persian Gulf.

My barge, the *Wimbrown 7*, was smaller, about 220ft by 85ft–and totally different from Norm's. Although my barge was smaller than the *Hercules*, it had two helicopter platforms, one aft and the other forward. That worked out great because we could bring over one or more of the MH-6s, then launch both the Nightstalker Task Force 160 birds and our own for joint operations together.

Our barge had TF117's AH-58 Warrior helos, the tiny gunships with the mast-mounted sight. They were wonderful birds, with superb pilots, and they didn't get the credit they deserved from the guys on Norm's barge, the *Hercules*, who had helicopters and crews from Task Force 160 *Nightstalkers* (the Army's special ops aviation unit). There was a lot of contention back and forth about just who had the best helicopter operation, but the AH-58s seemed to fly a lot of times when the AH-6s and MH-6s from TF160 wouldn't fly. We never had a problem with them, although one was lost after I left; an engine failed over the water and the crew had to ditch. But the two pilots were immediately recovered. I had a lot of respect for those guys and what they did.

These little gunships were highly classified at the time, with good reason–they were amazing little fighting machines, almost invisible on radar, with the latest in sights, sensors, cannon, and Hellfire missiles. The imaging systems, in particular, were extremely impressive; you could see detail miles away at night that you couldn't hardly see during the daylight with normal systems. And if you've seen the movie *US Navy SEALs* and the scene where the guys are able to see through walls . . . well, the AH-58 wasn't quite that good, but almost. (And since then unclassified systems have been demonstrated that actually *can* see through walls).

Our mission was to provide an escort service for the tankers and the warships as they transited the Gulf, up to the northern region where the oil terminals were. Normally, we launched the 65ft Mk III Patrol Boat (PB Mk III) for this job during daylight. When the weather kicked up, something that could easily happen in an hour, we could use the cranes to pull the boats out of the water and secure them on deck. That was handy. Then, when things calmed down (and that could happen in just an hour, too) we could promptly launch the PBs again and send them off in search of gunboats and pirates.

The helicopter patrolled, normally at night, using different routes and always hunting for the little speedboats. The enemy tactics basically involved hiding behind buoys and little islands–anything that could provide a little cover and concealment from our radar or observers in aircraft or aboard ship. Their boats were mostly home-made, with a kind of bath-tub shape, and were powered by nice Volvo marine engines. These boats generally mounted a ZPU-2 in the bow, an excellent Soviet 23mm cannon designed for anti-aircraft and ground targets. Some of the boats also mounted simple launch tubes for free-flight rockets

When a target vessel got within range, these little boats would sprint out, lob the rockets into the side of the hull, shoot up the bridge of the ship with the cannon, then make a high-speed run for cover. Ordinarily, this would have been quite effective. But we had learned a few things over the years, and after years of neglect, we were starting to get some really "high-speed" weapons for dealing with this kind of threat.

Our little helicopters were one of these new weapons. They were designed to be extremely quiet; the gunboat crews couldn't hear them unless the helicopters were within just a few hundred yards. At night, when the birds flew and couldn't be easily seen, the enemy basically didn't know we were out there until the bullets started tearing up their boat.

And while the enemy couldn't see or hear the helicopter, the AH-58 Army pilot and gunner had an *excellent* view of every detail on the water and along the shore. The AH-58 has a "million-dollar beach-ball" mounted on top of the mast; while the rotors spin below it, this housing stays still. Inside are highly sensitive, motion-stabilized sensors–a daylight TV camera plus a forward-looking-infrared (FLIR) thermal imaging system that provides excellent detail even at night. While radar provides a rough, general image of objects, the systems in the mast-mounted sight (MMS) allow inspection and targeting of small, distant targets in total darkness, through rain and fog. So we were able to pick out the bad guys, even when they were hiding behind pilings or buoys.

Silkworm Suckers

Naturally, they (the Iranians) wanted to get us, too. We had to move the barges quite often to keep them from setting up on us; they had radar-guided Silkworm missiles that could hit us, and we had the biggest radar signature in the Gulf! So we developed ways to counter that threat, one of which was something we called a "Silkworm sucker." These were great big radar-reflectors mounted on pontoons and moored around the barges. Although the barge provided a huge radar return, these reflectors were at least as good; coming back on the PBs from a patrol, we couldn't tell one from the other. Neither, of course, could a Silkworm missile, and that was the whole idea. Of course they were a hazard to navigation around the barges; one morning I awoke to see a minesweeper that had been alongside my barge refueling, heading south in the Gulf at about 10kt dragging one of the pontoon mounted reflectors behind that had become hooked on the sweeper's rudder.

Iran Ajr

Before we got the barges into service, back in 1987, our helicopters found an Iranian landing craft, the *Iran Ajr,* in the process of putting anti-ship mines into the Persian Gulf, in violation of international law and despite warnings from the United States. The ship was specifically warned to halt the mining by the helicopters. The *Iran Ajr* responded by firing on the helicopter and continued to put these huge mines over the side, into the water.

If the Iranians ever did a "lessons-learned" session on this incident, I'll bet they decided they'd made a BIG mistake. The helicopter fired a salvo of 2.75in Hydra rockets at the vessel. These rockets weren't the usual high explosive variety, but a type with hundreds of little steel "fleshettes" that literally nailed the enemy crew. This was the first and so far only (as far as we know) combat use of this rocket warhead; as the rocket approaches its target, the warhead pops open to dispense a cloud of sharp little steel darts that scream through the air with a frightening howl. These darts saturate the target, killing or wounding everyone exposed to them if the target is within the weapon's effective range–and the *Iran Ajr* was in range. Many of the Iranians on deck got skewered.

Then came a salvo of rockets with high explosive (HE) warheads; these damaged the ship, set fire to some fuel barrels on deck, and pretty much brought the Iranian proceedings to a halt. The crew abandoned ship.

While the birds circled overhead to keep an eye on the vessel, the SEALs hopped in a landing craft and dashed over (to the extent you can dash in a LCM-8) to execute a takedown of the *Iran Ajr.* The crew was captured without further resistance, although some of them played dumb and tried to escape in survival rafts–not an effective E&E technique in this case.

JTFME–NSWTU "PACIFIC"

About this time, 1988, I got orders to be relieved as Commander of SEAL Team Three and take command of Task Unit *PACIFIC* in support of the Joint Task Force, Middle East. Norm Carley had already gone over to take over Task Unit *ATLANTIC.*

We all knew it was going to be a tough deployment. The Little Creek staff was saying, "We can't leave our guys out on this austere duty for six months; they wear out so fast that we want to rotate them out every 90 days. The Coronado staff said, "We'd like to leave them over there for six months but we agree that this is a hardship tour, and we propose a 120 day tour." As it turned out, we West Coast SEALs served 120- to 140-day tours and the East Coast SEALs got 90–but they were recycled more often, so there was really no escape.

I felt the longer tour just made more sense. It took you a month to just get your bearings, then you got to operate at peak efficiency, and then the last month everybody naturally started anticipating going home. It seemed to me that the East Coast guys were only really good for about a month of peak efficiency while the longer deployment served by the West Coast SEALs produced about two or more months of peak efficiency. While this sort of thing might not seem very exciting, considerations like this–expressed in the form of policies and procedures–has a lot to do with how effective we SEALs are at completing the missions assigned to us. It is part of the story-behind-the-story of the US Navy SEALs.

CPO Jim Gray

If you only know about SEALs and the NSW community from the movies or from novels, you really don't get a good understanding of what goes into a SEAL mission. Before those dramatic few moments of combat (if any) come months or years of training and preparation, followed by weeks of planning and executing the mission itself. Lots of people are involved, some whose contributions are essential but who never get any glory. In the movies they appear as bit-playing extras–if you see them at all. In places like the Persian Gulf they were stars of the show, even if they didn't always get top billing.

One of these guys in the Persian Gulf was a guy named Jim Gray, then a chief petty officer, now a senior chief, who had a profound impact on me, even though I only met him toward the end of my career. Jim was, and still is, a reservist–a "weekend warrior" who normally works for another government department–who was called up for Earnest Will. Jim wasn't even a SEAL but a boat-driver; he skippered one of the PBs assigned to my barge which he subsequently nicknamed the Dragon boat. I'd been in command for about a month when Jim was rotated in to take over one of the boats.

Jim arrived full of questions and enthusiasm. The questions were really good ones and influenced the way we planned and operated. He had plenty of combat experience in boats and consequently had lots of ideas about tactics–good, sometimes brilliant ideas. Not only that, he fired up his superb boat crew, and they turned their PB into a glittering work of art–immaculate from stem to stern, weapons systems up and humming. He and his men clearly out-performed everybody else . . . including the active-duty crews!

I took a closer look at this guy, and it was obvious he was head and shoulders above everybody else when it came to operationally running that boat. He had combat experience in

Vietnam, doing the same thing, so it was no surprise that the weapons were in perfect condition, good to go. You could eat off the deck plates, too. Jim and his whole crew were all reservists, and that was a shock because we usually don't expect much from part-timers. Jim pulled these reservists together as a crew, then used them and the boat in tactically superb operations. He was teaching the *officers* in the boat units how to run the boats! Jim is mostly responsible for completely revising and enhancing the PB tactics in use at that period in the Gulf. That's an example of the kind of professionalism we need in NSW and sometimes find in unexpected places–a guy who has a profound influence on his whole command, on the command's combat operations, and who isn't either a SEAL or an active-duty sailor.

Persian Gulf Learning Curve

Every time we deploy someplace like the Persian Gulf and an operation like Earnest Will a learning curve is required of all of us, the commanders, the guys on the teams, the boat crews, and all the support people who help hold the spear.

As a commander of a task unit, I had a lot of issues to study and understand; I had to learn about the weather, about where we could and couldn't patrol, and about the "Q route" the tankers took transiting the Gulf. I had to know how to get in and out of Kuwait while escorting these tankers. I had to make sure my boat crews knew how to repair the boats out in the Gulf, under way, and during operations because nobody was available to do it for us; if you got a hole in the boat you had to be ready to patch it, right now, and get it moving again. If the motor mount broke, you had to fix it yourself and get on with the patrol. Everybody learned to be very good at this.

Interdicting the Iranian Gunboats was our offensive mission, but we had a defensive mission, too. Those barges were such big, fat, rich targets that nobody could miss them. The secret helicopters and the high-profile escort mission made us natural targets for both Iran and Iraq. So we set up a layered defense, beginning with the PBs who could screen the barges at great range. Our second line of defense was the helicopters; we could launch them against bad guys–if we knew they were coming our way. Then, we usually had a man-of-war nearby, often a fast frigate. Their long-range surface-search radar could pick up contacts at great range, and they'd provide a play-by-play commentary on activity in our operational area. They let us know when fighters launched from airfields inside Iran and Iraq, told us about possible gunboat movements far over the horizon and kept an eye on possible threats on the sea and in the air.

With this kind of defensive screen, I wasn't too worried about the gunboats, and I wasn't too worried about the aircraft (because there wasn't much I could do about that threat, anyway); but I WAS worried about the Silkworm missiles because we were such a big target and we were well within range. I was particularly worried about the possibility of a sneak attack from one of the many little fishing dhows working the reefs near our position.

These fishing boats were a real concern because they all ignored our signals to stand clear, often coming within 200 or 300 yards–easy range for small arms and RPG-7s that could have caused a lot of damage to our exotic little helicopter. I figured that, sooner or later, one of these things would pull a Beirut-style suicide mission and turn into us with a load of several tons of explosives.

To counter these threats we used the patrol boats and helicopters, plus a close-in defense supplied by a contingent of Marines. For airborne attackers we kept a Marine aloft on top of the hanger deck 24hr a day, armed with a Redeye (Stinger) missile, ready to fire if any enemy fighters got in range. And for surface targets, we also had a TOW missile ready to blow enemy ships out of the water. And finally we had 20mm Vulcan gatling guns that could shoot 4,000 rounds a minute–and cut one of the fishing dhows in half in a couple of seconds. This 20mm weapon was a system I had helped the Navy test in 1975, so I was delighted to have them on the barge; the projectiles had a high muzzle velocity, with plenty of HE warheads in the mix, and had an almost laser-like flat trajectory. With two of the Vulcan guns and several .50cal heavy machine-guns on each barge we could deal with any gunboat that managed to penetrate our screen. We had so many weapons systems and sandbagged bunkers on this barge that the hull started to be effected by a effect termed "hogging" or sagging at the fore and aft ends, with cracks beginning to appear in the hull plates. After that we were told by naval engineers from Naval Sea Systems Command (NAVSEA), "that's it–no more weapons on THIS little barge!"

A major incident almost developed out of our concern for security of our mobile sea base platforms. Our barges were classified. We did not even allow the AH-58 helicopter gunships out of the hanger in the daylight to be seen by satellites or passers-by. It was well publicized among the other nations' military units in the region that our platforms had a "no-approach zone" of 1mi radius out, either by air or surface. Even the Russians, while flirting with the approach angle, did not come into that radius.

The French, who were also out in the Persian Gulf to protect their shipping concerns in the region were attempting to re-establish diplomatic ties with Iran about the middle of my deployment time to the Persian Gulf. One day, my radar watch detected an airborne target coming over the horizon. We immediately set general quarters to position all personnel on the barge at battle stations. By the time I arrived at my position atop the helicopter hanger roof where the Stinger missile team was located, we could visually identify that a single attack helicopter of unknown identity carrying missiles was fast approaching our position. We attempted to reach them by radio, to no avail. We launched red flares to warn the helo off. We locked onto the helo with our Stinger system, so they had to know they were being set up to be fired upon if necessary.

As it came into range, and just before firing a Stinger in self-defense, the helo was recognized to be a French gunship. Despite our launching several flares at the helo to attempt to divert it away, the helicopter came within 50yd and circled the platform taking photos all around before departing back over the horizon. I announced the incident immediately to ADM Tony Less, our Task Force commander, who called in the French senior officer to explain that if it ever happened again, the US military would not be responsible for defensive actions taken by the security on the barges. The ironic thing is that within the next couple days, the French reinstated relations with Iran. We felt confident that the photos were part of the negotiations between the two nations since the Iranians had not been able to come close enough to see the platforms in the past.

Oil Platform Take Down

On 12 April 1988, the USS *Samuel B. Roberts* was severely damaged by a mine. The following day I took command of the barge; instead of a routine, four-day change of command, I got word that we were going to retaliate. Norm, who'd arrived earlier, got tasked with a take-down of an Iranian oil platform that had been converted to a fortress in the Gulf.

Norm had plenty of CT experience and was a natural for the job. He spent two days planning the op with RADM Tom

Richards, our planning group commander at the time (and prospective Commander of SPECWARCOM) in the mission planning cell.

Their plan was to send in a Navy destroyer and shoot up the platform with armor-piercing (AP) ammunition. This would scare all the enemy personnel on the platform, make them put their heads down, and let us come in with troop-carrying UH-60 helicopters to land on the helipad and put a bunch of SEALs on the rig to capture the bad guys–a classic "take-down" mission.

It was an excellent plan . . . but, in the grand tradition of war, somebody didn't get the word. Instead of the AP ammunition specified, somebody onboard the warships loaded up incendiary and HE. When the ships went in to fire up the platforms not only did it scare the socks off the bad guys, it set fire to the platform! The enemy had the good sense to jump in the water, but the platform melted down before we could put anybody aboard.

Welcome to the Persian Gulf, Part II

Well, no sooner than we recovered from *that* little adventure, the US Navy got into a little missile duel with the Iranians. I guess the Iranians resented the way we tried to take down their oil platform, so they sent two warships, a coastal patrol ship and a destroyer, out against our surface units. These both launched missiles at our ships; our ships fired missiles in return. Their missiles missed, ours hit. Both the Iranian ships were sunk, and several smaller craft were damaged. Now they were REALLY mad! You won't find this documented in any official source, but they launched Silkworm missiles on our barges!

Remember, I had just taken over command of this barge. I had been learning everything I could about our defenses and was up on the Stinger platform on the crane. Our commodore from Coronado, CAPT Ted Grabowsky, happened to be visiting that day, and he was up there on the platform with me as we got word from the destroyer, the USS *Gary,* (the name is only coincidence) that we had Silkworm missiles inbound on us!

"What do you want me to do?" he asked.

"Get in the PBs and get them away from the barge–stand by to pick up survivors!" I told him. "If this thing hits us we will have a lot of casualties."

The missile was, at first report, 46mi out and closing fast. The Silkworm is a Chinese-manufactured, radar-guided anti-ship missile with combat-tested reliability. It is designed to blow a big hole in a big ship. It would have made a real mess of us.

I launched the helicopters, too; they could help with a rescue effort and were extremely high-value targets besides. We went to general quarters; the commodore took charge of the boats, people scurried all over the place, going to their stations. A master chief asked me, "What do I do? Should I put on my life preserver and jump over the side?"

"No," I told him, "nobody jumps; we don't know where it will hit, or IF it will hit. Nobody jumps until after it hits us!"

The young Marine with the Redeye missile was standing next to me; he was shaking. "What do I do, sir?" he asked.

My mouth went dry. I was NOT a happy camper at this moment. We were getting the range on the inbound missile from the destroyer: "44mi . . . 42mi . . . 40mi . . ."

"Treat this just like a training scenario," I told the young Marine, "try to lock on that thing, and if you do, tell me 'lock on' just the way you were trained. I'll tell you to fire."

Like a good Marine, he said "Yes SIR!"

At 18mi the USS *Gary* began to engage with their 40mm guns and anti-aircraft airburst rounds. Now their radar showed TWO Silkworms, close together, streaking toward us. After firing on the missiles, the frigat lost radar contact with them. Then there they were again, range 12mi and closing! The skipper of the USS *Gary* was doing a great job, firing chaff and doing everything he could to defeat the missiles before they hit us. And he must have done something right because as the two missiles closed on us, their guidance systems seemed to fail. I saw one go by us, then hit the water nearby. Norm saw the other missile decoyed into a cloud of chaff fired by the USS *Gary,* then plunge into the Gulf on the other side. Norm's Redeye gunner actually had a "lock-on" on the missile but couldn't fire because the destroyer was in the line of fire.

So the Marine didn't have to fire the Redeye, the master chief didn't have to jump in the water, and we didn't have to get rescued. The commodore came back and said, "Boy, that was exciting!" The master chief took off his life jacket. But it was a close call and another lesson learned about combat operations in the Persian Gulf. Well, actually, the lesson wasn't quite over.

First, we all recovered and relaxed a bit. That evening we were watching "Robocop" down in the mess deck when general quarters sounded again. "*Forty enemy gunboats closing, range 35mi,'*" came the report from the USS *Gary.* At about 30mi the destroyer started "pinging" the inbound targets with their fire-control radar. The Iranian boats took the hint and immediately made a 180deg course change. That was more than enough excitement for most of us for one day. We went back to our movie–and then general quarters sounded AGAIN! This time it was a flight of six Iranian F-14s inbound on us.

The commodore turned to me and said, "I am NOT taking those darn boats out again; this time I want to stick around and see what happens on the barge!" Of course, having him around wasn't such a good idea–he ranked me and would probably want to take over . . . that's why I always sent him off with the boats! But the fighters turned away, too, and we finally got to watch the end of the movie.

A couple of weeks later we got another lesson on operations in the Persian Gulf. ADM William Crowe, then Chairman of the Joint Chiefs of Staff, came out to talk to us about the incident. The admiral, a very gracious gentleman and leader, talked to us about our role in the Gulf. "If those guys attack you," he said, "we will respond with force." Well, the Iranians already HAD used force against us with those Silkworm missile launches; we all saw them, and we knew we'd been attacked. But in the days since the attacks we'd been getting told that–despite what we all saw–the Silkworm attacks were just a false alarm . . . we all imagined them somehow.

Tom Richards, never shy about speaking up, asked the admiral, "Sir, could you tell us how these Silkworm missiles we all saw didn't attack us? We have the radar tracks, recordings, and we all saw them."

"No, Commander," I think ADM Crowe said, "there weren't any Silkworms fired at you guys. You see, *if there had been*, according to the threats we made to the Iranians, we would have to respond with some serious damage. Well, we aren't quite ready to go in and do that . . . so we don't acknowledge they did anything to merit a response."

Life on the Barge

I have never really needed much sleep, so I often prowled the ship at night, talking to the watch-standers, asking how they are getting along, what they're seeing and doing. The lookouts really had an important job because we'd occasionally encounter a floating mine that had broken loose from its mooring chain and was drifting in the current. This prowling around at night was pretty motivational: they never knew when their commander would show up and that tended to keep them quite alert.

But the first night I tried that the crew didn't yet know about my nocturnal tours of the duty stations, or maybe even that there had been a quick change of command between the other CO and myself. In order to go aloft, where the missile stations and the lookouts were, required a climb up through the hangar, then outside on a kind of "monkey-bar" ladder arrangement, then up the side of the hanger and the crane. That first night I climbed up to the platform and was taking a look at the Redeye and the guns. One of the Marine watch-standers came up and challenged me with "What are you doing up here?"

I replied, "Oh, just looking around."

"Well, this is a firing station," he said. "You aren't supposed to be up here!"

"Really?" I said. "Why's that?"

"Because it's OUR station!" he told me with a fair amount of vehemence and pride.

"Well," I told the sailor, "it's my station too."

"You aren't assigned to this station!"

"That's true, but since I'm the CO of the barge, I thought it was *probably* okay," I told him.

"Jeeze, I'm sorry, sir, but I've been here for four months standing night watches and the other CO never came up here!" And that's how the crew discovered that I might drop in on them in the middle of the night.

Barging Around the Gulf

The Silkworm attack and all the subsequent excitement actually did us a lot of good. It got us doing frequent damage control exercises that could have saved a lot of lives if we ever actually took a hit.

So this was a very busy time for me, the embarked SEALs, and all the crew. We were running missions around the clock; we had a briefing for each mission, plus a approval-briefing (my job) before that to make sure the guys understood the rules of engagement and the mission objectives. We launched patrols at unpredictable hours every morning, launched the helicopters every night, also at varying and unpredictable hours. That meant I had to be listening to a helicopter patrol briefing at midnight, wait for the launch at one, then be up again at 0400 to hear the debriefing when they got back.

Another thing that kept us all awake was the frequent violation of our 1mi exclusion zone. All kinds of boats and ships blundered into our zone, and each was a potential threat. When anything got within just 2mi I had to be notified, and we came to alert. Any unidentified helicopter *anywhere* on the horizon also brought us all to a high state of alert because it, too, could attack us. All this meant a 24hr day for a lot of us. I usually got 3hr at night, then another hour right after lunch.

The time did go fast on the barge. The men were restricted to a postage-stamp size piece of steel in the middle of the steamy Persian Gulf waters for months without getting off except for helicopter and PB patrols, if they were so lucky as to be assigned to those units. Mailcall from the every other day or so delivery was one of the most sought after moments for each sailor, marine, or airman. The weather was hot, the time was lonely for all, but the deployment was gratifying. Distractions were minimal, and each individual felt integral to the overall operation. The lessons learned throughout the Earnest Will operation should be preserved and drawn upon whenever the concept of mobile sea-basing permits.

CHAPTER 10

BUD/S and Training Issues

I've been through some tough programs in my life, in high school, college, post-graduate work, and in the military, but nothing holds a candle to my experience at BUD/S. BUD/S is the most difficult–and most rewarding–achievement of anything I have ever attempted. Other programs might be easy if you're really smart, or if you're a natural athlete, but no matter how good you are when you come in the front gate at the Silver Strand side of the amphibious base in Coronado, the instructors will find something that just takes you to your limits, and beyond, and humbles you. It is supposed to be the toughest program in the free world.

A lot of the program is mental. It is a brutal, calculated, scientific program to develop people–or eliminate them. They start you off at a tough, challenging level, then they "grow" the students up from there. If you have any kind of physical problem, like bad knees, that problem will be aggravated and you will have to leave. But if you can avoid injury at BUD/S you will be conditioned until you can handle the physical challenges of the program; the physical part is just a small part of BUD/S, though.

The major part of BUD/S is the mental stress and strain, the emotional brutality the instructors impose on you. The instructor's job is to push you until you quit, or they see that you've got the will to keep going when things get bad. And if they really want to, they can make *anybody* quit!

Take the "rock portage" evolution for an example of the kind of physical and mental stress designed into BUD/S. This event involves taking the boats out at night, then bringing them in to land on the rocks right in front of the Hotel Del Coronado. The rocks are extremely slippery; the surf can be high, and the conditions are appallingly dangerous. I had one classmate break his back right next to me. Guys broke ribs and legs on the same rocks I was landing on, at the same time. Those injuries are just part of the program, and part of the stress for everybody who doesn't get hurt on one of these "evolutions." When you watch somebody break his back on the rocks and you have to take your boat out and go through the process all over again, the effect is to make you think and to be more cautious. It also makes you pay extra close attention to what the instructor is telling you. When he says, "Paddle HARD!" you do what he tells you instead of trying to just ride the wave into the rocks.

But why even put people through this dangerous training in the first place? The rest of the Navy and the armed forces are careful to never put trainees in such hazards–and would severely discipline instructors who allow injuries to occur. At BUD/S they are not only tolerated, they are virtually encouraged. Why?

We are in an inherently dangerous business. When a SEAL squad comes in on an enemy beach, they never really know where they'll have to come ashore; it might be on nice, soft sand, a rock, or a cliff; it pays to prepare for the worst. Then, a nice soft beach shows footprints and rocks don't; that can be important in combat, and rocks may be the best place to come in. Rocks are obviously a less likely landing spot to the enemy, too, and are less likely to be guarded while the beaches would be heavily patrolled. That's part of the reason for rock portage.

By the time BUD/S students get to this part of the program, they ought to know how to avoid injury by doing the landing properly. They've learned all about the inflatable boat, small (IBS); first how to paddle it, then how to get through the surf during the day. Then the trainees will make landings on the rocks during daylight. They learn to work together as crews. Night landings on the rocks are a test; people who fail get broken bones and are never seen again. Everybody knows how this works. It is scary. And the fear is part of the program.

At night you can't see the rocks ashore, or the wave you're about to catch, but you can hear the booming surf on the rocks, the hiss of the water retreating, over and over again. You listen to this, knowing you have to go in; it is *frightening.* You can hear the instructors ashore screaming "Get him out from under there! Get him out!" The waves might be only 3ft high, but you think they're 10ft high because of the night and the fear. I was lucky; my class had to only deal with waves up to about 6ft, but the next class rock-portage was conducted during a winter storm with waves of 8-10ft high. They had lots of terrible injuries.

Now, you're thinking, *How awful! They shouldn't do this!!* But SEALs think it is a wonderful part of the program. It is a graduation exercise with real-world tactical value. People have had to do this sort of thing in past combat, and they'll have to do it again. It develops important skills. And it weeds people out.

There were guys in my class who said, "I am NOT going in there! You can let me off right here and I will swim ashore!" We had three whole boat crews quit in one night! Of the 180 people who started in my class, only about forty five graduated, and we lost lots of guys on the nights we went in on the rocks.

We say there are three reasons you graduate from BUD/S: you're either crazy and don't care; you're trying to prove something to yourself; or three, you're trying to prove something to somebody else. In my case, it was the last–I wanted to avoid at all costs having to call my folks and tell them I didn't finish something I started. It wasn't that they pushed me to go–my dad thought I was crazy for trying–but it was the admission of failure that was unacceptable; that kept me going.

Well, I almost did quit the night during hell week that we did rock portage, but another guy in the boat said, "Aw, let's give it until the end of the evolution and see what happens." And once we got through that first night run in on the rocks I felt great and was ready for the next portage. That's the way you survive BUD/S.

You don't know this as a BUD/S student, but the instructors are careful about when and how they do these things; if it is an extremely cold night, for instance, they might back off a little. The students never see this, though. And if it is a nice, warm, moonlit summer night they will push harder, to even up the strain. There is a logic–invisible to the student–to the system.

The only way to get through BUD/S is the same way a recovering alcoholic gets through life: one day at a time, one evolution at a time. The first day one of the more famous instructors, PO1 Vince Olivera, told us, "If you think you can't go on, remember that a lot of people have been through this before. Second, the guy alongside you is suffering just as much as you are. Third, you go through one step at a time; there may be a thousand steps, but each day brings you ten steps closer to graduating." He was right, too, because much of BUD/S is mental–it is so easy to quit, so hard to keep going. The individual steps are, by themselves, often not all that tough . . . it is the unrelenting, increasing pressure that is tough.

Welcome to Coronado, Mr. Smith

BUD/S operates with a higher intensity and with different procedures than other Navy training programs, a process that begins just about the moment you arrive. There is no gradual period of adjustment, you join your class immediately.

Although the real training hadn't even started, we had been introduced to the water by the friendly, ever-attentive staff, and already lost one class leader, a lieutenant, after just two days. The BUD/S staff liked to crank up the heat on newcomers, just to see if they'd stick, and a lot turned right around and left. We were out in the bay–BUDS at that time was located on the bay side of the amphib base–we were standing in the water, singing songs and shivering until the instructors sent us off to a different form of torture.

Ray Smith (Admiral Smith now, LTJG Smith then) checked in at the quarter-deck and filled out the usual paperwork.

"LTJG Smith, you are now the senior man in this class," Ray was told.

"That's nice," he said.

"Lt. Smith, *you need to go lead your class!"* he was told. The instructor pointed to the rest of us thrashing around out in the water.

"But they're in the water!" Ray objected.

"Right. HIT IT!"

"Yes, Instructor!" Ray replied and jumped in with the rest of us, still in his dress blues.

The O-My-God Course

The obstacle course, or O course, is one of the first instruments of torture you encounter at BUD/S. It is a series of what looks like playground-structures-from-hell. You run a circuit of these obstacles, climbing, hopping, jumping, crawling from one to the next. When you arrive at BUD/S you run the course, doing your best, for time. Then, you have to keep bettering that time and your last time to stay in the program. It was one of the worst parts of BUD/S for me, and I will give you an example of the kind of stress we experienced.

The trainees were out on the O course one day, and a guy named Jimenez, a little overweight, was on the slide-for-life station. The station requires a long transit along an inclined heavy rope, about 20ft up on the starting end and 8ft up on the finishing side; the station is about two thirds through the course, and by the time you get to it your hands are always in bad shape, and they hurt. Jimmy (as we called him) got about half way across, then fell. "Get back up there and do it again" the instructor roared. He did it again, and fell again. He had to repeat the process again. This time he fell from about 15ft up onto his hands–and got up in tremendous pain. He ran up to an instructor, saying, "My hands! I hurt my hands!" he said.

"I don't care if your hands hurt or not," the instructor said. "Get back up there and do it right!"

Jimmy got back up and hooked his elbows around the rope and negotiated the whole station that way. He even finished most of the course, without the use of his hands. The last station was the monkey bars, supervised by then PO Terry Moy. "I can't make it!" Jimmy said.

"You get through here or start over!" Moy told him.

Jimmy screamed and cried, but he got through the bars. With no sympathy whatever, Moy sent him over to the corpsman with the ambulance who took him to the dispensary. Both wrists were broken. But he didn't quit BUD/S–when the bones healed he finished with my class. And he was part of NSW for just about as long as I was, until he died recently of cancer. That's the kind of mental toughness the instructors were looking for–and found in "Jimmy" Jimenez.

Log PT

Log PT (physical training) also tests toughness, but in a different way from the O course. There is no way one man, or even three, can lift one of those logs, no matter how big and strong you are. But if everybody works together as a team, you can get through it. If one guy wears out or doesn't pull his share, the whole team loses. The logs are about 16in in diameter and about 16ft long. Each seems to weight about five tons, but in reality are probably about 300-400lb. The trainees are given orders to lift them into various positions such as on their right shoulder, left shoulder, hip level, and other positions that could not be accomplished if each person doesn't pull his own.

TJ Runs and Burnout PT

The normal PT is pretty challenging and gets more so as you go along, but once in a while the instructors throw something extra at you, just to keep you from getting the idea that you might get through the program. One example occurs shortly before Hell Week, a little jaunt called the TJ run. It begins with 2-1/2hr of "burnout" PT: jumping jacks, pushups, eight count body-builders, knee-bends until your muscles feel like they will catch fire. Then, when you're ready to collapse, it's out to the beach for a 14mi scamper on the strand, up to the North Island fence on the air station, then back down all the way to the Mexican border fence. You get a drink of water and an orange at the fence, then you run back to Coronado.

Now, 14mi isn't that far to today's marathoner athlete, but of course the instructors don't make it that easy, even discounting the effect of the burnout PT. Whenever anybody started to straggle and need a rest, we all had to get into the ocean and wait for him. Then it was out again, and off down the beach–loaded down with sand and salt water in your boots and fatigues. The sand abraded the skin, the salt water made the abrasions sting. By the end of the run most everybody was bleeding and blistered in places more than their feet. Then two days later, before anything gets to heal completely, Hell Week begins.

Hell Week

No other place in the armed forces tolerates anything approximating something SEALs celebrate and revere, the brutal experience we call Hell Week, and it all starts out with a bang! It is something you never forget; our Hell Week began with us in our racks, pretending to be asleep. The instructors tossed in smoke grenades and there was a lot of screaming. The preferred wakeup call today is the M60 machine-gun firing blanks, with just as much screaming.

We were mustered and dressed and then sent out to the "Grinder" where BUD/S students do PT. Everybody had to lay on the concrete and then the instructor turned a fire hose on us. This was in October, and it might have been in Southern California, but it was COLD anyway! Once we were nicely chilled, they got us up and ran us into the water over on the bay side of the island.

"Okay, once you guys can form a nice, straight line from the pier out into the bay we will be done with this evolution!" they said. Sound like a piece of cake? Well, there is always a nice current past this pier, ebbing or flowing. At that point our class had nearly 200 men in it, all wearing a life jacket, swim trunks, and a determined, chilled, uncomfortable expression. We were all strung out along a line–but it sure wasn't straight. We were freezing! And there was no way we could get ourselves in a line that was straight enough for the instructors, even though we tried for a couple of hours in that frigid water. Finally, after they got us miserable, they said "Okay, enough of that, let's try something else." And the class was lighter by a few people even then.

Hell Week is actually very structured, although it doesn't seem that way to its victims, and it is far better now than it was back then. We've brought in stress physiologists, nutritionists, and other specialists to help get the most out of the experience. We made some things harder, others easier. But the structure of BUD/S is to put the really dangerous evolutions, the things that can break bones or really hurt people, during the first two days, Monday and Tuesday, because you're still functioning well and you still have strength and judgment. After that, all they really want to do is to keep you moving and awake all the time. You think it is tough at the time but actually you're just doing "light duty" PT. I maintain that if you can get past Tuesday night the rest of Hell Week is a piece of cake–relatively. You won't even know what's happening to you because you're totally numb or delirious. The hard part is while you're getting cranky, you're still functional, while the instructors are still putting a lot of physical demands on you. We all feel a certain amount of pride for going the whole week, but actually I don't even remember much of anything of the last three days.

One thing you do during the last days of Hell Week is the Treasure Hunt; you'd get a clue that required some reasoning ability, then you and your boat crew paddle off to where you think you're supposed to go. If you find the right spot someone will hand you a new clue. Then you move off to the next place, and that goes on all night long! You paddle, and you walk, and then paddle some more, all over the place. And that boat goes with you everywhere! If you aren't paddling it, you carry it on your head! Well, that boat isn't light and the tall guys got unfairly loaded; the short guys had to try to find something to do their share. Here's where you start to see real leadership; the boat crews either pull together, or they fall apart together. And when one guy decides to quit others often follow, sometimes three or four at a time.

The Coronado Quick Weight Loss Program

As hard and mindless as it all seems, the instructors are careful to make sure you get plenty of food and eat often. Hell Week burns phenomenal calories so there is a big breakfast, a huge lunch, an immense dinner–and then MIDRATS, midnight rations. It seems at times that all you're doing is carrying that boat back to the chow hall for another meal. Even so, you're likely to lose weight.

Just about everybody will get cellulitus, the breakdown of the cell wall that results in infections. And some of us still have the condition, many years later, as a result of Hell Week. The week is very hard on the body, inflicting damage that doesn't always go away.

The Hell in Hell Week–the Cold Water Swim

I have always been a good swimmer and was teamed early in the class with an Olympic gold medalist butterfly champion, Fred Schmidt, in BUD/S for the swims. Swimming long distances wasn't the problem, it was the frigid ocean water. After forty minutes in that water I had nothing left; I couldn't even stand up for quite a while after crawling up on the beach. BUD/S has a reputation for inducing hypothermia, something I experienced often during my training. Often I would have to crawl out on the sand on elbows and knees as the hands would not work. Someone would have to assist me in taking off the fins, pulling on the boots and tying them, because my hands were so cold so as to not even function. Then ten minutes later we would be running and sweating again.

While many of the swims were tough, the toughest was the five-mile swim off San Clemente Island. The seas are almost always choppy or with large swells. The kelp can tangle you. Trying to swim with a gold medalist swimmer was even more challenging. To him this was a "walk in the park," but to me, the combination of cold and Fred's constant effort to make me go faster to keep up with him made the swims not fun.

The Rest Period?

After you're good and tired, in the middle of the night, they let you lie down on the beach, but not to rest. "Look up in the sky," they say, "see that bright star? Everybody watch that star for a while!" Of course people start to fall asleep; when they do the ever-friendly and attentive staff wake them up and have them stand in the cold surf. "Go! Get up! Hit the water!" Nobody lasts long. I can still hear that instructor asking, "Mister Stubblefield, you aren't sleeping, are you?"

"Oh, no, sir!"

"Yes you were! Get in the water!"

Lies My Instructors Told Me

One of the instructors, a chief named Jones often made us do the "duck walk" so we nicknamed him Mallard. We were standing out in the water, freezing. Mallard Jones came up with a tape player. "Are you all cold?" he asked. We assured him that we were *very* cold, thank you, sir!

"Well I have an idea for something that should warm you up. Everybody pair up!" We paired.

"We're going to have a dance contest. Dancing ought to warm you up. And the best couple will get a beer!" Wow, a beer–that was quite a reward. So he started the tape player and we started dancing, right there in the water. It must have looked hilarious to the instructors because we were out in the water up to our waist, in our uniforms, waltzing. Chief Jones gradually eliminated all the couples but one–the winners! And, much to our surprise, he actually produced a can of beer and let each guy drink half.

But what do you think a little alcohol does to somebody who's been awake for three or four days? Both the guys were quickly basket cases! They were worthless for hours, and they were virtually unable to perform effectively for several hours.

Anybody who is still around after four days of this kind of treatment starts to hallucinate. The instructors have been here themselves and know what is happening. They watch to see if you're still trying to function, that you try to remember what you are supposed to be doing. Your mission might be simply to paddle from one buoy to another, but if you haven't slept for five days your mind starts to do strange things. I remember then ENS, now RADM,Tom Richards' boat going around in circles instead of from one buoy to another. In fact, I seem to remember him trying to jump overboard.

"Thank Goodness It's Friday" at BUD/S

By Friday, the last day of Hell Week we were down to about six boat crews. Tom Richards, Ray Smith, Jon Smart, Fred Schmidt, Nick Walsh, and I each had one, and that was all that was left. Our last major evolution on that Friday afternoon started with the instructors drawing a big circle in the sand; "Everybody get inside that circle!" they ordered. We got inside. "Okay, the last man left inside the circle will, along with his boat crew, get to secure early after this drill and be finished with Hell Week today; everybody else has to keep going through tomorrow! Hit it!" The brawl began.

At first we tried to work together, as boat crews, but that quickly deteriorated to a free-for-all. Now, I have never been a big bruiser, and I relied on hiding out, but we got down to just three guys left in the circle–Ray Smith, Tom Richards, and me. Both of them are big lunks, and I was hiding, pinned under both. I was exhausted, and so were they. I was hoping for a chance to bounce one of them, though, while they were wrestling each other. Tom Richards was lying in the sand–still inside the circle, but pretty much hors d'combat. One of the instructors, PO1 Moy, wandered over with a boat paddle and started "motivating" Tom by digging sand and pouring it on his head.

Richards, who was then about 205lb of solid muscle, leaped up, threw Ray Smith right out of the circle and took off after Moy as fast as he could go, with mayhem on his mind. Tom had a tactical problem, though; he couldn't really see a thing because his eyes were full of sand. He chased Moy (a very large and accomplished fighter) quite a ways down the beach even so, until the other instructors tackled him and calmed him down. I thought then and still believe Moy was in serious danger if Tom had caught him.

That left me still in the circle–but the instructors, in their normal perverse way, decided under the circumstances that nobody really qualified, so none of us got to secure. That was just one part of the hell of Hell Week: they'd build you up, lie to you, then let you drop.

Then, on Saturday morning, it was all over. I really don't remember too much about the details of my Hell Week at this point; the last few days were and still are a blur. But we were finally secured, went back to our barracks, showered and slept for a few hours. Then we got some chow, went back to sleep again for a while. Within a day or so we were all back to a normal training routine.

AAR for Hell Week

As brutal as it is, I hope we never lose Hell Week as part of BUD/S or the SEAL program. It is valuable, just the way it is. It is a program that has been changed and adapted over the years, toughened in some ways, and weakened in others. It is harder on people mentally now, but a little less stressful physically since the students started getting 1-1/2hr sleep each night. The original program kept you awake and moving from Sunday midnight until the following Saturday morning, a real physical challenge.

It is just about as hard on the instructors as the students. They have to be there all the time, running along with the students. They watch closely to make sure nobody gets badly hurt. The evolutions don't have any real tactical training usefulness, but they allow the staff to see how you perform under extreme stress. Do you have the stamina for SEAL missions? Are you somebody who quits when you're tired and uncomfortable and harassed? Do you lose your temper and fly off the handle? Can you remember what you're supposed to be doing and continue to make an attempt to complete your mission? That's all Hell Week is, a weeding process that removes all but the very most healthy, committed, focused men.

I have always felt that when Hell Week ends, those who survived the ordeal will, in all likelihood, be the same ones that will be standing at the end of the class for graduation. For the most part that holds true. There is always the possibility that one or more will be dropped for injury, or for a safety violation, or in very rare cases for lack of ability to perform as a SEAL is expected to perform. But the first phase which ends when Hell Week is secured, marks the point at which most of the men can feel they will likely make it to graduation day. Of course the instructors can give the impression that this simply isn't so.

Phase Two–Getting the Payraise

The instructors do appear to take it a bit easier on the class the week following Hell Week. It gives the trainees a little time to heal the blisters and raw skin produced by the grueling week prior. But the classroom work picks up. Whereas the majority of the time in First Phase is spent on physical activities, the remaining two phases will emphasize more cerebral activities while maintaining a good dose of physical efforts along the way. The next two phases will emphasize two primary skills: basic operational skills such as shooting, demolition's, patrolling, mission planning and other skills which will become a daily routine in the life of the new warrior; and diving skills. After all, if we are to keep one foot in the water, it is reasonable to expect that we will have to become adept in that liquid, whether it be salt or fresh.

The land warfare phase was a big item to most of us in the old days. It essentially meant the point where we could begin to earn more money for doing the things we were trained to do. The big day came when we were taken to the "demo pit" on the Silver Strand to be subjected to explosive simulators and smoke grenades going off all around us while we were trying to navigate our way across the line stretching over the pit–which was filled with scummy green water that had been sitting there growing all sorts of things that would make a microbiologist proud. But despite the subjection to new strains of critters, we did walk away from the evolution with the designation of demolition trained and thereby a significant payraise in all our monthly incomes.

Nowadays, the trainees are taken to San Clemente Island to the luxurious camp which was placed out there to keep the sounds of the explosions going off from upsetting the residences along the Silver Strand. Actually this camp is a primo training facility that is a far cry from the days when this trainee was a young tadpole. In those days, the camp consisted of a couple steel Quonset huts which housed the students, supplied a chow hall, and permitted mission planning and briefings. It was so infested with mice that we had to shake out our sleeping bags and shoes before getting in them as we learned the first evening from a revealing experience by Tom Richards. When it came time to hit the rack after a long day of classroom lectures on demolitions, he threw off his clothes and all 205 pounds of him leaped into the Navy issue mummy bag only to let out a blood curdling yell and leap out faster than he got in. Standing on the cement floor, he shook out a mouse that had about as much fear of him as he seemed to have of it. There was also the night that (then) Petty Officer, First Class, Instructor Chuck Shinners came back from the only drinking facility on the island only to trip in the chow hall when he went in to find a midnight snack and have six mouse traps snap on his hands in the dark room. His yelling and hand waving as he ran outside with the traps stuck on his fingers woke up the entire camp.

There were other niceties on the island that the instructors arranged for us to enjoy our stay. We all, at one time or the other, took an "iron butterfly" flight up Mount Saribachi, the seemingly long pinnacle of rock and cactus that rose up behind the camp. The flight entailed putting a big airplane cargo pallet on our back, similar to a weird set of butterfly wings, and be timed by the instructor to run to the top of the mountain and back on the well-worn trail that went up and down the slope. Crashing on takeoff or turnaround was not unusual on these flights.

Then there was the practice of doing an approved set of dips on the "horizontal dip bars" before we could enter the chow hall for a bite of good Navy chow. Actually it did serve to pass the time and to strengthen us for the flight with the iron butterfly.

We also got to swim the longest swim of the entire training course out there. I think it would be fair to say it exceeded five miles; two and one half out from the piers and two and one half back. The swim was kept from becoming boring by wondering how deep the water was under you, how many sharks might be circling just below the water's surface, and when the local bull sea lion was going to come up to perform its territorial biting act on our bodies to remove us from its brood of females cavorting in the kelp beds.

But our time on San Clemente did serve to provide us the basics of mission planning, using demolitions both on land and in the water. The exercises that culminated the time out there included conducting a night over-the-beach combat operation that included firing lots of blank ammunition and having a controlled demolition of a target. The final problem entailed doing a classic beach reconnaissance from boats offshore to see where the beach obstacles and mines were along the surfzone; then returning and planting live charges on them and blowing them up. I recall some of them being as deep as 40ft and tying in the detonation cord using the old breath holding technique that we have traditionally used since WWII.

Third Phase - The growing of Gills

Once we returned from San Clemente Island we encountered a whole new class of instructors. They didn't seem to want to spend so much time harassing us along with the instruction; in fact, it seemed to be a sort of quiet approach to ensuring we learned how to dive. They started us out in the swimming pool with open circuit SCUBA gear not unlike that used by the sports diver, except in our day, the Navy was still using the old double hose regulator that made us look like Lloyd Bridges on the TV program "Sea Hunt." Once they felt we were competent enough, they moved us out to the bay and we ran compass courses in the muddy bottom against the support LCPLs that they cast and retrieved us from. First, day swims, then night swims. Then it was back to the pool to learn the mixed gas and closed circuit SCUBA systems. At that time we learned on the MK VI and Emerson rigs. These have been replaced by the MK 15/16 mixed gas units and the Draegar LAR V closed circuit units respectively. Each are far superior to their earlier brethren. This was the easiest time of the entire course for me as I had been a SCUBA diver since age twelve in the cold waters of Montana and a certified civilian SCUBA instructor for the previous several years.

We learned to dive on these units, to swim accurately against a target from under the water surface, and to go deep when required without getting into medical problems. We practiced placing inert charges on target vessels with the dream of someday having such an operation tasked to us for real. To date the only ones to fulfill this dream is the detachment led by Norm Carley when he sank the Noriega patrol vessels in the Panama Canal in 1989.

Somewhere near 180 trainees began Class 54 but only about 45 tadpoles were standing in formation the day of graduation waiting to become Frogmen and SEALs. After that ceremony, we all reported to the UDT or SEAL command that the Bureau of Naval Personnel directed us to. We knew we would all have to attend one more three week training course–jump school at Fort Benning, Georgia–in our first few weeks as soon as slots opened up, but at least we were finally out of BUD/S and assigned to a team. For me that first assignment was SEAL Team One and the beginning of a challenging career.

CHAPTER 11

The Final View From the Outside

When I entered the Navy Reserve Officer Training Course (NROTC) in the University of Idaho in 1965, it was in part a way to defer the inevitable draft notice, and in part a way to get into the military with a commission. By the time I graduated and received my commission and orders to UDT Training, I was excited but still had in mind that this brief endeavor would be over after satisfying my 3yr obligation. At the end of those 3yr I was having a lot of fun and agreed to a tour in Korea as the UDT advisor; but before leaving for there I applied for and received a regular commission. By the time the tour in Korea was over, it still seemed fun, and I made a decision that as long as it remained so I would stay on active duty. Along about the 12yr point, I recognized that I was only eight years from being retirement eligible. Things were going well in my career, and I was determined that regardless of what was in store, I would remain to the 20yr mark.

The 20yr mark is the point, where, if one stops, he gets 50 percent of his base pay (equivalent to about 33 percent of his actual pay and benefits) in retirement checks until such time as he assumes room temperature. Whereas if one stays for 30yr, he will get 75 percent of his base pay or about 50 percent of his actual pay and benefits. If one plans to enter the job market, there is more time to enjoy or at least experience a second career if one enters it after 20yr in the military versus 30 yr. At 14yr, I also began to recognize that my personal forte was serving in the field with the troops–not behind a desk. I was fortunate enough in my career to enjoy lots of field time and then a run of prime assignments from 1986 to 1990 when I retired. But I knew that from about the 18yr point on, I would be too senior to get operational assignments, and more importantly, would be entering a career period that required being politically correct to compete successfully. At best I figured I would make Navy CAPT (O-6) and get command of a NSW Group or equivalent, and the rest of the time be placed in staff positions. Besides, it was already becoming evident that the military was drawing down, promotions were slowing, obligated service time for promotions was extending, and to achieve a 30yr career was becoming more difficult.

Every individual, sometime along his career, has to realize that if he doesn't decide his own destiny of when to throw in the towel, the Navy will do it for you. Even the Chief of Naval Operations is told when to go home. When I recognized that, I made the decision to retire at 20yr. Exactly 1wk prior to my first look for promotion to CAPT, I submitted my retirement request, almost a year ahead of my actual retirement. It allowed me the opportunity to begin planning for my next career and be better prepared for the inevitable culture shock. Now having experienced this, I can strongly recommend to every military man to think ahead about life after uniform. I quickly learned that high school, college, and the Navy had not taught us one of the more important things, financial planning for the future years; and a 20yr retirement will not support life. Work was not only desired, but required.

I didn't want to remove myself from the subject area that I was most familiar with and experienced in–naval special warfare operations. I knew that my community had provided me with an incredible twenty years and if I could find a way to sustain an income and yet instill many of those lessons learned back into the community, it would be doubly fulfilling. While that hasn't proven totally possible, at least a majority of my work since retirement has involved equipment procurement programs and development of doctrine and tactics for the special operations folks and also in related commercial endeavors. I have learned repeatedly that at least there is still plenty of adventure available for those who want to experience it after retirement. In fact, in just five fast years, there have been enough thrills and excitement to ponder writing about some of those adventures someday.

Index